Make No Mistake

William Hicks

A WINGHAM BOOK

Canterbury

First published in 1994 by
Wingham Aviation Books, Padbrook Lane,
Elmstone, Kent CT3 1HF

ISBN: 0 9521404-1-1

Typesetting in Times and Raleigh
by Stephen Bloomfield (Graphics)
Roughton Road, Cromer, Norfolk.

Printed in Great Britain
by The Cromwell Press Ltd.,
Broughton Gifford, Melksham, Wiltshire.

Preface

Make No Mistake exposes to the basic rules of grammar and acceptable word usage more than two hundred examples of English language errors, distortions or deviations. The aim is to aid anyone who has the occasional doubt when writing an application for a job, a school essay, a business report, a university thesis, an advertisement, an office memorandum, or a letter to a friend. It may also clarify points in simple terms for students from other countries or at home who are learning English as a second language.

William Hicks is not an academic grammarian, although he consulted several. He is a journalist who has edited hundreds of thousands of words on national and regional newspapers, trying always to communicate to the reader in sentences properly punctuated and understood at a glance. His newspapers included the Daily Mail, Daily Express, News Chronicle and Eastern Daily Press (Norwich). After Fleet Street, he became a senior lecturer at Harlow Technical College, running full-year journalism courses for students with two or more A-level passes. That experience, plus the laments of HRH the Prince of Wales and successive Secretaries of State for Education about the decline in use of the English language, brought his fingers to the keyboard to write these pages.

He is a member of the Queen's English Society, but recommendations and opinions in this book do not necessarily reflect every stand taken by the society. For nine years he was a member of the Sports Council, where he was chairman of the Public Affairs' Committee and wrote two extensive official inquiry reports that went to the Government.

THE LAST WORD (pages 178 and 179)

The case for an English language authority

CONTENTS

Acknowledgements

Much outside knowledge and experience were tapped before this manuscript went to the printer. Not all advice offered was taken — to be expected since the English language has many personal preferences and interpretations. If the content is criticised, the author emphasises that the responsibility is his, entirely.

Thanks are passed especially to Sylvia Chalker (grammarian, author of the recently published *English Grammar Word by Word,* by Nelson), Geoffrey Kitchin (linguist, lately tutor at English language school for foreign students), Brenda Brooks (English language scholar), Professor Andrew Wilkinson (University of East Anglia), Philip Bloomfield (editing), Dr Robin Hicks (University of Bath), Christopher Hicks (IBM senior computer consultant), Judith Brooks (Further Education English tutor), Cherry Newman and Peter (Joe) Barrett, former lecturing colleagues at Harlow College, Peter Bagshawe (South African author), Stephen Bloomfield (format and production), Carolyn Midgley (senior secretary), Jean (author's wife), who tested every draft for easy, at-a-glance understanding, and the *Oxford English Dictionary,* which was always within reach.

Posthumous acknowledgement: Jimmy Dingle, long since dead, was head of the village school at St Stephen's within the ancient borough of Launceston in the county of Cornwall. His knowledge was encyclopaedic and his teaching in every subject excelled any enjoyed or endured later at grammar school and part-time colleges. At 10 we could spell accommodation, separate and the other spelling conundrums. And we knew about predicates.

Make No Mistake

A mistake in the English language corrected today should ensure that misused or misspelt words will be right when written tomorrow. ***Its a pity*** becomes **It's a pity,** ***the principle speaker*** becomes **the principal speaker** and **separate** is not spelt ***seperate.***

That is the concept behind this book. But the following pages offer more than a catalogue of corrected errors. Correction without explanation is as futile as a balance sheet without the company's name. The alternatives suggested to words, phrases and grammatical deformities are given reasons to make them acceptable in school, business, the professions and to writers of personal letters.

Examples chosen for *Make No Mistake* were collected from reports, memoranda, newspaper and magazine articles, as well as business and private letters. Disputes, such as "Should it be **all right** or ***alright?***", were not bypassed; the case for each side is given. A few recommendations, however, oppose spellings and interpretations now accepted by many as *Standard English (e.g., ***alright*** is not approved here; **all right** is right).

The experience of lecturers, secretaries, managers, parents, students, journalists and examiners was used to make up a picture of everyday mistakes. The focus is on five main areas:

1 – Punctuation.

2 – Misuse of words and faulty construction of sentences.

3 – Knowledge of simple English grammar.

4 – The apostrophe.

5 – Spelling.

A minority of people, including some teachers, believe that punctuation, grammar and spelling are of little or no importance as long as the message is

**Standard English is taken broadly to be the language of the educated, as taught to the foreigner. Changes evolve, new words are created and old ones are forgotten, but the grammar of half a century or more remains for most of us.*

understood. Creativity and imagination, they claim, require no rules. This book is not for them; for their victims, perhaps. The 400 million people worldwide who speak and write English should not be taken into the backstreets of dissent to seek the right word or phrase from "letter-louts".

Oxford English Dictionary spelling and Standard English grammar enhance creative and imaginative writing and give authority to any communication, whether it is for public or private attention. To be considered, too, is the foreigner who is learning the language and is baffled when trying to translate the words of a non-conformist.

Secretaries of State for Education in the British Government have scorned the way English is often written. Their strictures induced, even demanded, a new emphasis on spelling, grammar and punctuation. One minister may have exceeded reasonable expectations, except from the brightest, when he insisted that, by the age of seven, children should be able to:

1 – Spell correctly.
2 – Write compositions using capital letters, punctuation, tenses and pronouns correctly.

The Prince of Wales has often called for conformity and preservation of language standards. *"We have seen the abandonment of learning the rules of grammar and the parts of speech as being boring and irrelevant",* he has said.

The Northern Examinations' and Assessment Board reported in 1993 that standards of basic English among the previous summer's A-level students were appalling. Many from a nationwide total of about two thousand schools were said to have been unable to write in sentences or punctuate properly, making errors so elementary that one would have expected such faults to have been eliminated in primary school. The report attracted wide publicity in national newspapers.

Examples from history candidates included "Henry hated ***waist***" and "Royal expenditure had reached ***gastronomical proportions***". English language examiners said the distinction between a comma and a full stop appeared to be quite unknown to many.

Accurate, clear writing is dependent on a grammatical base. That does not mean rote learning of all the terminologies. Failure to recognise words as ADJECTIVES or NOUNS is a serious deficiency. But the ability to define a SUBJUNCTIVE MOOD clause or an INTRANSITIVE VERB is seldom needed – never by most of us.

The word GERUND, for instance, is probably unknown to 98 per cent. of the population. But this verbal noun can be reduced to simple terms – i.e., the part of a verb ending in **-ing** and used as a noun. Her **cooking,** his **writing** etc. flow naturally from the pen without thought of grammatical identification.

Dr Bernard Lamb, reader in genetics at London University, carried out a survey for the *Queen's English Society* across different subject areas in 17 representative U.K. universities. His findings, published in 1992, were astonishing.

Up to 40 per cent of undergraduates were found to be poor at spelling normal English words and scientific words, more than 60 per cent did not have an adequate grasp of grammar and 25 per cent could not punctuate satisfactorily. Typical mistakes were to confuse **sight** with ***site,*** **affected** with ***infected,*** **accept** with ***except*** and **principal** with ***principle.***

Dr Lamb, in press interviews, was quoted as saying that he had witnessed a severe decline in English standards among his own students, with bad English leading to bad genetics. Scientific terms misspelt could be potentially lethal, he said.

His survey confirmed an embarrassing fact, seen in many places, that writings are often corrected by foreigners who have been taught English spelling, grammar and punctuation more rigorously than in many of our schools.

In 1992/3, BBC Radio 4 produced with flair and wide appeal a series of programmes that examined modern use of the English language, under the title *Word of Mouth.* From thousands of letters the producers compiled their listeners' Top Ten Horrors:

1 – Problems with countability (PLURAL VERB following SINGULAR or COLLECTIVE NOUN), ***amount*** used in error for **number,** ***majority*** applied to uncountable nouns, ***their*** used to replace **his** or **her** etc.

2 – ***Different to*** used in place of **different from.**

3 – The use of ***like*** to mean **as if.**

4 – ***Disinterested*** mistakenly used to mean **uninterested.**

5 – Word confusion. ***Flaunt*** for **flout,** ***infer*** for **imply,** ***mitigate*** for **militate** etc.

6 – Jarring sequence of tenses. "The government ***may fall*** if the vote ***had gone*** against them."

7 – ***On behalf of*** mistakenly used for **on the part of.**

8 – ***You and I*** wrongly used.

9 – Misplaced apostrophes (***Christma's's*** was one awful example).

10 – ***Decimate*** used in error to mean devastate – it technically refers to a reduction by one tenth, not to one tenth.

Examples of the unacceptable

(a) Mistakes appear in unexpected places. The Government's DVLC, Swansea, sent their printed driving-licence renewal form to a motorist with ***effect*** instead of **affect** and posted the same form to his wife four months after their attention had twice been drawn to it. The offending extract:

> 14. Have you now or have you ever had any disability or medical condition which could *effect* your fitness as a driver either now or in the future?

(b) The Girobank invented a new word in a letter to the author: "***Whatsmore,*** there is no annual fee..."

(c) A college of higher education, which has since become a university, advertised in a national newspaper for ***Principle lecturers.*** It was extraordinary that the fault was not picked up in the advertisement department; it would not have been an editorial responsibility.

(d) Every day we hear on radio and television sentences such as "I shall ***try and repair*** it", distorting the credible "I shall **try to repair** it". Most editors insist on "try **to** repair", although in speech many people contend that **and** applies emphasis, giving us the meaning **"I shall try and I will repair it".**

(e) A letter under the signature of a university's vice-chancellor, submitting a report on the English language to the Secretary of State, wrote – "...encourage every child to the ***fullest*** effect in speaking, writing, listening and reading".

If a box is **full,** can it be ***fuller*** or be the ***fullest*** in the house? No. ***Fuller*** and ***fullest*** are mistakes, but are heard, seen and accepted every day. It is fair to report, however, that a distinguished grammarian, who wishes to be anonymous, supported the vice-chancellor's use of ***fullest*** in a letter to the author, in these words:

> Justification of the word ***fullest*** is to be found in usage of the language. For more than 200 years, ***fullest*** has been attested in standard English prose, in such phrases as ***fullest capacity,*** to the ***fullest extent, fullest good wishes*** etc. In questions of correctness, final appeal can be made only to what is actually used, and not what is to be found in text-books or dictionaries.

The opinion of an academic grammarian must be respected, but *Make No Mistake* concedes neither logic nor sense when words that are absolutes have their meanings enlarged. ***Fullest, emptiest, most perfect*** and others *(see page 53),* when written for emphasis, can be excused only as colloquialisms.

(f) Examples of crippled English were seen in an English council's package sent to hoteliers and others, canvassing advertisements for a holiday guide. The apostrophe was ignored:

...this *years* Guide. ...the first *nights* accommodation

...*womans* magazines. ...this *years* show.

...this *years* brochure.

...a new series of local interest leaflet entitled "***Lets*** (Let's) Look At".

Its (It's) a fairer way of treating the visitor to the district.

The apostrophe has obviously already lost its importance to someone – possibly one who writes to many members of the public and whose examples of English are there for others to copy. Those were not the only mistakes in the circular:

Demand for the 1992 Guide has ***lead*** (led) to a reprint.

...and it is likely that if no commission is paid hotels etc. will ***loose*** (lose) bookings.

From the same council, a letter, signed by the deputy chief executive, sent to many ratepayers, read:

You were recently sent a Council Tax Survey Form for ***it's*** (its) completion and return in a prepaid envelope.

Misspelling

Spelling ought not to be a problem, provided a dictionary is kept close at hand and there is the will to use it. There are so many exceptions to basic rules that writers with a lifetime's experience sometimes pause to ask themselves: Is it **receive** or ***recieve?*** And: Is it **preferred** or ***prefered?***

Publishers of repute allow few errors to pass into print, but promotional letters, leaflets and brochures with elementary misspelling drop through the letter-box every day.

The higher levels of education do not guarantee accurate spelling. An Inland Revenue tax inspector had difficulty with **transferred** and **correspondence.** In one handwritten sentence she wrote ***transferd*** and ***correspondance.***

For a month, this notice in metre-high letters outside a Norfolk farm-shop could not be missed: Strawberries ***organicly*** grown. At least a hundred children passed it every day to and from school. Mistakes as well as corrections are copied. The correct **organically** is probably unknown to some of them now.

Differences in spoken and written English

The differences in spoken and written English have to be acknowledged. A speech or private conversation may be colloquial and in a local dialect – not to be condemned, because some of it, at any rate, may be part of that area's heritage. Words spoken in Norwich or Newcastle may be foreign to the Cornishman, and nobody would wish them to be lost, as many have been. But one of the Government's education ministers put that statement in perspective when he objected to giving ethnic and regional dialects the same weight as good English, adding: *"At the end of the day, people have got to be able to communicate effectively across the country".*

A speech or conversation is invariably in shorter sentences than in an essay or written report. An article by a distinguished author in *The Times* some years ago included a sentence of 94 words! A student, asked to read it aloud, became flustered then silent within ten seconds.

Difficulties confront foreigners learning the language when they try to translate into script slovenly words and phrases they have heard. Equally important is the influence such spoken English has on children, especially when sitting in front of a television screen.

Television, in particular, has probably had more to do with the decline in language standards – not only in the United Kingdom – than any other source. News reports may be exonerated in part, although the political editor on one channel persistently said "***Neither*** the Prime Minister ***or***...". And, on radio one day, we heard ***"more newer"***, then ***"more earlier"***, and later ***"more harder"***, each from a well-known politician.

Children who hear Standard English spoken daily in their own homes will intuitively apply the rules of grammar without necessarily knowing about them, especially if they have been encouraged to read good literature, whether found in books, the best newspapers or magazines. They will also have learned that written English is more formal than speech, with more time to consider choice of words and phrases. In its puristic form, BBC news readers' scripts probably attract a majority vote of approval among those who try to defend traditional English.

The campaign against those who believe that all is well with their language, provided the intended sense of a communication is understood, has gathered momentum. But the language non-conformists were greatly encouraged in the mid-eighties when a British examining board reported that candidates sitting A-level modern language examinations need not always write or speak in sentences, that answers in incorrect English could gain full marks, and that communication was sometimes more important than grammar. That notion is discredited here.

A candidate, for example, would get full marks from them for this answer in a comprehension exercise:

> He told them that he had ***stole*** (stolen) the watch from a judge and that he stole the ***broach*** (brooch) from his lawyer while he was embracing him in court.

Changes in structure and new words appear from time to time, generated mainly in speech. They are acknowledged in these pages; but the grammatical foundations, as laid down in text books for half a century, must remain, or international English will break into a multiplicity of dialects. **Brooch** (an ornamental clasp) will never become a **broach** (a roasting spit or church spire).

Make No Mistake's list of the most common errors:

1 – Indiscriminate punctuation, particularly in placing a comma where a full stop or other long pause is required.

2 – Use of ***its*** instead of **it's** and ***it's*** instead of **its.**

3 – Confusion over use of the apostrophe, with little or no knowledge of its importance or its purpose.

4 – Spelling of separate, accommodation, occurred, preferred, recommend and occasion.

5 – Plural and singular mixed. "The test (**singular** noun) on the ten samples ***were*** (***plural*** verb – wrong) satisfactory."

6 – **Neither** and **either** used with ***are*** instead of **is.** "**Either** George or Tom **is** (not ***are***) here." "**Neither** of the two men **is** (not ***are***) capable of doing the job." *(See exceptions, page 94).*

7 – Neither with ***or.*** "***Neither*** George ***or*** Tom turned up", should be "**Neither** George **nor** Tom turned up".

WHEN IN DOUBT – Re-write it. That's the answer to conflicting advice, difficulty or doubt. Get rid of ugly words and clumsy phrases, even if they appear to be right. Always pause before committing a guess to paper. Reach for the dictionary.

A noun gives name to place, person or thing,
From *Wint* to *wing,* from *Ripon* to *ring.*

A pronoun stands for noun already seen,
Like *he* for Eddie, and *it* for bean.

A verb will tell us what's to come,
To *strum,* to *drum* or to *hum.*

An adjective describes a lonely noun,
Red roses, *bad* lad, *lovely old* town.

An adverb answers How? When? or Where?
Walk *carefully,* come *now,* don't stay *there.*

A preposition points to time or place,
Through Pontypool *at* noon *to* Upper Race.

A conjunction words and phrases links,
Not claps *or* clangs, *but* clinks *and* jinks.

An interjection pops up with lusty shout,
Hello! Hurrah! There's a lot about!

ANON

Parts of Speech

Mistakes are acknowledged with less doubt and corrections better understood if, in some cases, the grammatical background is provided. Parts of Speech, and The Sentence chapter that follows, give definitions to which the reader of the later Wrong/Corrected pages may wish to refer.

What is **a Noun?**
a Pronoun?
a Verb
an Adjective?
an Adverb?
a Preposition?
a Conjunction?
an Interjection?

The number of parts in the English language has varied at different times. Articles **(the, a/an)** in some manuals have been defined separately, often as DETERMINERS. Here they are classed as adjectives, making eight parts in all. A few books omit the INTERJECTION as a part of speech.

Nouns

The word noun means name. A noun, therefore, is the name of something – anything – classified here under four headings:

COMMON *(names of people or things)* – book, sailor, carpet.

PROPER *(names that belong only to particular persons, places or things)* – Harry, London, Smith, Hamlet, Tuesday.

ABSTRACT *(name of some quality, action or state)* – sleep, acting, happiness.

COLLECTIVE *(names of groups of persons or things)* – crowd, committee, team, herd, army.

Plurals – Nouns are singular when denoting one object or person (book, Englishman, garden). Plurals to represent more than one (books, Englishmen, gardens) are created in the following main forms:

1 – The addition of **-s** converts most nouns, including names, into the plural:

arms, athletes, buckets, beetles, colleges, files,
ornaments, lambs, months, scholars, trains, stones,
weeds, Mr Brown/the Browns, Mr Smart/the Smarts.

2 – Words that end in **-sh**, **-s**, **-ch** and **-x** pluralise with **-es** added:

bushes, wishes, thrushes, classes, gases, kisses,
hutches, birches, churches, foxes, boxes, taxes.

The same change comes with nouns that end in **-z**, but such nouns as whizzes and buzzes are rarely written.

Names of people also fall into this category:

Mr Jones/the Joneses, Mr Hix/the Hixes, Mr Rush/the Rushes,
Mr Gibbs/the Gibbses, Mr Buzz/the Buzzes

3 – When nouns end in **-o**, the normal practice is to add **-es**:

potatoes, negroes, heroes, volcanoes, tomatoes, echoes.

Exceptions: solos, ghettos.

But the rule adds only **-s** when a vowel precedes the final **-o**:

cameos, radios, folios, studios, cuckoos, tattoos.

4 – Many nouns ending in **-f** or **-fe** change to **-ves** to become the plural:

half/halves, life/lives, loaf/loaves, thief/thieves,
wife/wives, wolf/wolves.

Others add a simple **-s**:

cliffs, roofs, safes, chiefs, fifes.

5 – Nouns ending in **-y** preceded by vowels add **-s** for the plural:

boys, toys, keys, valleys, trolleys, trays.

Exceptions, seldom written:

soliloquy/soliloquies and colloquy/colloquies.

When a consonant precedes **-y** the plural becomes **-ies:**

baby/babies, lady/ladies, territory/territories, fly/flies, story/stories, army/armies, variety/varieties.

Exceptions (names): the two Henrys, the Marys, the Hardys.

6 — The middle of a few nouns changes to denote the plural, usually with different vowels:

man/men, foot/feet, goose/geese, tooth/teeth, mouse/mice.

7 — Some nouns in common use do not change for the plural:

sheep, deer, swine, salmon, grouse, cod.

8 — Two nouns become plural with **-en:**

child/children (a variant with an extra **r**), ox/oxen.

The normal English rule now applies for the plurals of many foreign words — **consortiums** (not *consortia*), **librettos** (not *libretti*) — but *memoranda* for **memorandum** and *fungi* for **fungus** remain.

Pronouns

A pronoun is a word that stands for, but does not name, a person or thing. Authors of grammar manuals classify them in various ways. They are broken down here as follows:

PERSONAL pronouns are used

(a) **First person** — when a person speaks or writes about himself/herself **(I, me)** or with others **(we, us).**

(b) **Second person** — a speaker denotes the person or persons to whom he/she is speaking **(you).**

(c) **Third person** — used to denote the person or thing **(he, him, she, her, it)** or persons or things **(they, them)** being referred to.

John Smith writes a letter. He does not start "***John Smith found*** Trevor Jones most helpful" but "**I found** Trevor Jones most helpful". The personal pronoun is used in place of the nouns John Smith. The next sentence could be: "**He knows** the place well and **I trust** him".

DEMONSTRATIVE pronouns point to something *(a noun)* but do not name or describe it – **this, that, these, those.** "This is a lovely area."

Used with a noun, they are DEMONSTRATIVE ADJECTIVES: "I saw that doctor."

REFLEXIVE pronouns refer back to a subject – **myself, yourself, himself, herself, itself, oneself, ourselves, yourselves, themselves.**

He hurt himself when he fell off the ladder.

RELATIVE pronouns are such words as **who, whom, whose, which, that, what.** They take the place of a noun already used, to avoid repeating it when additional information is needed. We could write:

I drive the car. The car is ten years old.

Instead, we would probably write:

I drive the car **which** is ten years old.

OR The car **which** (or **that**) I drive is ten years old.

INTERROGATIVE pronouns: **Who? Whom? Whose? Which? What?** They ask such questions as "Who broke the cup?"

POSSESSIVE pronouns show possession: **mine, his, hers, ours, yours, theirs.**

This house is **ours.** That car of **yours** should be scrapped.

OTHER (INDEFINITE) pronouns include: **everyone, everybody, everything, someone, anything, none, many, few, another.** The full list is long, known to grammarians as QUANTIFIERS – they all indicate quantity.

Verbs

A noun (e.g., Frogs) written alone is not a sentence. It needs at least a verb to complete it (Frogs **croak**). A verb says something about a person or thing – an action, event or state:

(a) What the noun or pronoun does, did or will do.

Frogs **croak.** He **raved.** Harry Brown **will survive.**
Godfrey **edits** a newspaper. He **broke** a new glass.

(b) What the noun or pronoun is, was or will be.

Ted **is** manager... **was** manager... **will be** manager.
Sylvia is kind. She **looked** sensible.

TENSES – A verb changes its form (**run** to **ran, eat** to **ate**) or its ending (**jump** to **jumped**) or has the support of an AUXILIARY VERB (**I shall run**) to indicate:

(a) The time of an event or action.

I **played** the piano. I **play** the piano. I **shall play** it.

(b) Completion or partial completion.

I **had played** the flute. I **have played** the flute.
I **shall have played** the flute before you arrive.

(c) The on-going nature of an action.

I **am playing** the flute. He **is looking** for his son.

A summarised guide to tenses is provided to take the reader through these pages, starting with the simplest form:

Present tense: **I manage** the farm. Past: **He kicked** the dog.

Future: **They will repair** the machinery.

Taking perfect to express completed or partly completed action, we have the second stage of tenses:

Present perfect: **I have sued.** Past perfect: **I had sued.**

Future perfect: **They will have sued.**

Use of the auxiliary verbs **shall** and **will,** known as helping verbs, has moved forward from the old grammatical rule which insisted that (a) **shall followed I and we,** and (b) **will followed you, he, she, it and they.**

The practice now in speech is for the voice to convey meaning and emphasis. As a result, **will** predominates. But writers recognise that these auxiliary verbs have two meanings:

(a) To express the future simply.

I shall/will go tomorrow	We shall/will go tomorrow
You will go tomorrow	You will go tomorrow
He/she/it will go tomorrow	They will go tomorrow

(b) **Shall,** in the first person, **implies promise** – "I shall go to Ayr today" – although **will** is stronger.

Shall also **offers** – "Shall I open the door?" – and **suggests** – "Shall we sing?"

In the second and third persons, **shall denotes determination, threat or promise** – "You (or he, she, they) shall be told tomorrow of the committee's decision".

Will implies willingness in the first person – "I will send you the picture you admire".

In the second and third persons, **will can carry exhortation and assurance;** sometimes a threat. Willingness becomes determination – "Tom will resign, ignoring every plea".

The future may be indicated without shall or will:

> **I am seeing** her next week. **I am going** to visit him tomorrow.

The INFINITIVE is the basic form of a verb, being an action not related directly to a *SUBJECT and normally preceded by to – to run, to have run, to be running.

To split an infinitive – "***to carefully examine*** the damage" – used to be censured and in most cases is still wisely avoided.

The PRESENT PARTICIPLE of verbs ends in **-ing:**

> I am **smoking.** We saw the thief **running** away.

The PAST PARTICIPLES of regular verbs end in **-ed** (talked) or **-d** (liked). Irregular verb endings include **-t** (wept), **-en** (broken), **-n** (blown), **-ne** (gone) and sometimes without a changed ending (cost), or with a changed vowel (swum, won).

A TRANSITIVE verb has an *OBJECT: "The girl plays **the piano**". The act of playing is not confined to something the girl is doing; she is linked to the piano.

An INTRANSITIVE verb denotes action, but not on an object. It expresses the state of a SUBJECT: "This boy **speaks** well".

Some verbs function as either transitive – "Ken finishes work today" – or intransitive – "Ken's work finishes today".

An ACTIVE VOICE verb is one in which the subject performs the action of the verb:

> The editor sacked the chief reporter.

A PASSIVE verb has the subject receiving the action of the verb, without changing the meaning:

> The chief reporter was sacked by the editor.

*See page 19 for grammatical definitions of SUBJECT and OBJECT.

Adjectives

Adjectives can describe a noun or comment upon it. They limit a noun to a particular quality, quantity or category.

There are different motor cars. Some are **new** cars, some are **old** cars, some are **fast** cars, some are **rusty** cars, some are **unpopular** cars, some are **red** cars, many are **automatic** cars and some are **expensive** cars.

When words such as **new, old, fast, rusty, unpopular, red, automatic** and **expensive** precede a noun, they are adjectives. And, of course, they are used after verbs such as **be, become, seem** – "It is rusty. It became rusty. It seems rusty".

COMPARATIVE degree – When two cars or two groups of cars, are judged for speed, the adjective makes a comparison. **Fast** becomes **faster. Slow** becomes **slower.** Two simple examples:

A happy man. A **happier** man. Big task. **Bigger** task.

SUPERLATIVE degree – When three or more cars, or groups of cars, are judged for speed, the adjective is upgraded to **fastest.** So we have:

A **fast** car – one. The **faster** car – of two.

The **fastest** car – of three or more.

Most adjectives of one syllable add **-er** (e.g. faster) for comparatives and **-est** (e.g. fastest) for superlatives:

shorter, shortest	poorer, poorest	fiercer, fiercest
larger, largest	weaker, weakest	lighter, lightest

For adjectives of three or more syllables, the word **more** in front usually makes up the comparative and **most** creates the superlative. We do not say ***unpopularer*** or ***unpopularest*** but **more unpopular** and **most unpopular.** Beautiful becomes **more beautiful** and **most beautiful.**

There are problems with two-syllable words. We write **prettier, cleverer, gentler** and **narrower,** but **more** and **most careful, most frequent** and **most private.**

Some adjectives are irregular. For instance, **good** becomes **better,** and **better** becomes **best.**

Several words that were once lumped together with personal pronouns can be classed as POSSESSIVE ADJECTIVES: **my, his, her, its, our, your, their.**

Thank you for the loan of **your umbrella.** That is **his pen.**

ARTICLES – As in many dictionaries, **the, a** and **an** are placed here under the heading of adjectives.

The is known as the DEFINITE ARTICLE. "The boat" refers to a specific boat – identified, identifiable. **The** can also be used with a comprehensive meaning:

The pen is mightier than the sword.

A/An are known as INDEFINITE ARTICLES. "A boat" and "an oarsman" often mean any boat and any oarsman. But **a/an** can also be specific even though indefinite:

A boat I once rowed almost sank.

An oarsman told me about the disaster that befell him.

Adverbs

An adverb qualifies or limits the meaning of verbs, adjectives or other adverbs, often answering How? When? Where?

George swims. Does he swim **well** or **badly?** George swims **well.**

Herbert speaks **slowly.** He walks **quickly.** The race starts **here.**

The criminal was **severely** punished. I paid the baker **yesterday.**

Adverbs may also place extra emphasis on adjectives or other adverbs. Examples:

Fred has **very** heavy loads to deliver. Ivy plays golf **extremely** well.

Adverbs may be separated into four groups. Examples:

1 – **Manner** *(How?):* Confidently, accurately, beautifully, sweetly.

2 – **Place** *(Where?):* Everywhere, below, inside, here, there.

3 – **Time** *(When?):* Often, never, now, soon, yesterday.

4 – **Degree:** Only, very, nearly, almost, quite, far, so.

Some adverbs are the same as adjectives – same spelling, same pronunciation, different meaning. That gives us a word such as **round** to be used as a noun, a verb, an adjective, an adverb and a preposition. **Hard, early** and **daily** are adjectives and adverbs, as written here:

Our craftsmen work **hard** *(adverb).* They use **hard** wood *(adjective).*

I arrived **early** *(adverb).* I want **early** payment *(adjective).*

Prepositions

Many people, when asked what they know about prepositions will say: "Don't end a sentence with one". In conversation, we are likely to hear:

> The letter didn't arrive at the address it was *sent to.*

instead of

> The letter didn't arrive at the address **to which it was sent.**

That rule has been modified by common use. **About,** for instance, is a preposition. Not many would say (correctly):

> The condition of the car he bought gave him something **about which to be furious.**

In writing that would be normal, but eight out of ten of us when speaking would say:

> The condition of the car he bought gave him *something to be furious about.*

A preposition is normally followed by a noun or pronoun. It denotes the relationship of one thing, or what a thing is or does, to some other thing. Example:

> George peered **through** the window.

George's peering is related to the window and is expressed by the preposition **through.**

Prepositions relate mainly to position, place or time:

about	above	across	after	against	along
amid	among	around	at	before	behind
below	beneath	beside	between	beyond	by
during	from	inside	in	into	near
of	on	out of	outside	over	to
under	until	up	with	within	without

Conjunctions

A conjunction joins two clauses, groups of words or single words. *(Clauses – see page 20).* Most commonly used are: **and** and **but.**

> The band played, AND the people danced.
> The band played, BUT the people did not dance.

Commas are placed before the conjunctions in those examples because the change of subject becomes easier to follow.

Other common conjunctions include: **or, if, because, since, as, unless, except, though, although, after.**

It is important to remember that two or more subjects connected by **and** normally take a plural verb:

> The car and the lorry are subject to speed limits.

There are exceptions. Bread and butter will be available in a restaurant. Bread and butter looks plural but it has a singular meaning when referring to a piece of food, and the words can be hyphenated into a singular bread-and-butter.

Interjections

An INTERJECTION is an exclamatory word or phrase that does not form, gramatically, part of a sentence. Examples:

> Oh! Alas! Hallelujah! What a pity!

THE EIGHT PARTS OF SPEECH

The	young	farmer	reluctantly	
adjective	*adjective*	*noun*	*adverb*	
agreed	to	the	deal	
verb	*preposition*	*adjective*	*noun*	
although	we	said	the	sheep
conjunction	*pronoun*	*verb*	*adjective*	*noun*
were	a	bargain.	Hurrah!	
verb	*adjective*	*noun*	*interjection*	

The combination that makes a sentence

A sentence is a group of words that expresses a thought, which could be about Mr Evans, the farmer, or his haystack. It must have unity, a oneness, related to a central idea, starting with a capital letter and ending with a full stop, question mark or exclamation mark.

Every sentence can be divided into two parts:

(1) The words that name the person or thing about which action follows – i.e., the SUBJECT.

(2) The words that say something about the name – i.e., the PREDICATE.

We write "Rainstorms are forecast". **Rainstorms** is the subject and **are forecast** the predicate. In longer sentences:

Subject	Predicate
Many heavy rainstorms	spoilt our holiday this year.
The new headmaster	takes up his appointment today.

Some verbs make sense when linked to a noun, because they report an action that has nothing to do with anything else:

Dogs **bark.** The boiler **exploded.** He **died.**

If we write "Philip rode" the sense is not complete. We then write "Philip rode the horse".

When the noun is placed after the verb in this way to show direction of the action, it becomes the OBJECT of the verb. And there we have the frame of a sentence:

Subject – Predicate – Object

taught with tenacity as a basic grammatical concept in schools years ago.

The forms of the verb **to be** are overwhelmingly the most commonly used of any verb. Sentences using them will have a SUBJECT:

John is. **I** am. **Mary** was.

But they cannot have an object. We cannot **are** something else, in the sense that we can **eat** something. Often it is necessary to follow a form of the verb **to be** with a word or words to complete the sense:

The girl in the back row **is beautiful.**

Johannesburg **is not a capital city.**

The word or words that follow in these cases are called the COMPLEMENT, because they complete the sense of the verb.

CLAUSES – Many sentences consist of more than one group of words, each known as a CLAUSE. This one has four:

If the house is sold | I shall give you £5,000 |
even if the full price is not obtained |
although we shall wait a little longer.

The main fact in that sentence is

I shall give you £5,000.

That is the MAIN CLAUSE. Each of the three other groups has a subject and a verb and is a SUBORDINATE CLAUSE. They are dependent on the main clause for meaning.

PHRASES – A phrase falls short of a clause because it is a group of words which has no subject and predicate. It passes for a single part of speech. Examples:

He will be here *(then the phrase)* in a minute.

I could see the Alsatian coming *(then the phrase)* through the gate.

THE WORK OF THE WORDS IN A SIMPLE SENTENCE

She will never find the boy; he runs very fast across the fields.

She: *Personal pronoun,* denoting a person without naming her.

Will find: *Transitive verb,* telling something about the person *She,* and denoting an action that passes on to an object.

Never: *Adverb* modifying the verb *will find* and indicating when action will take place.

The: *Adjective (the definite article)* linked to and pointing to the noun *boy.*

Boy: *Common noun,* being the same of something, which in another sentence could be dog, book, plumber, woman.

He: *Personal pronoun,* denoting a person without naming him.

Runs: *Intransitive verb,* telling something about the person *he.* It indicates an action that does not pass on to an object.

Very: *Adverb* of degree, modifying the adverb *fast* that follows.

Fast: *Adverb* denoting the manner of the action; it modifies the verb *runs.*

Across: *Preposition,* showing that *he* has to do with the fields.

The: *Adjective (the definite article),* joined to and pointing to the noun *fields.*

Fields: *Noun,* the name of something.

The Apostrophe

Two uses – one with problems

The apostrophe is often ignored, misplaced or misused. Some believe it should be abolished; even more have abandoned it, because they do not understand its importance. The entrance hall to a town hall has a direction sign:

► **Cashiers** office

Is there **one** cashier or are there **two or more?**

The apostrophe tells us. That simplest of examples shows its main purpose. It will be **-'s** for one (cashier's) and **-s'** (cashiers') for two or more. There are two basic uses:

A – Contractions

An apostrophe indicates a missing letter or letters in words and phrases as in:

(i)	**wouldn't** (would not)	**he'll** (he will)	**I'll** (I will)
	I'm (I am)	**you're** (you are)	**it's** (it is, it has)

Those examples are spoken but seen little in print, except **it's** and when conversation is reported. In print we see:

(ii)	one o'clock	rock 'n' roll	will-o'-the-wisp

Apostrophes adapt to many uses. We refer to the '90s (1990s). We write "There are three e's and two n's in the word sentence". Three es and two ns might puzzle readers.

B – Possession

1 – The apostrophe is evidence of possession (Sarah's flat, a firm's lorry). It is placed before the -s when the word is singular (Sarah, a firm), and before plural words lacking an -s (men's). In abbreviations, MP (Member of Parliament) collects the apostrophe for MP's constituency, as in UNESCO's budget. Examples in the singular:

Bob's book.	Bill's pen.	Mary's child.
The doctor's surgery.		An aircraft's wings.
A town's pavements.		The farmer's fields.

All seven can be re-written to explain the meaning in the most elementary terms but, with one exception, they make ponderous reading:

The book of Bob.	The pen of Bill.	The child of Mary.
The surgery of the doctor.		The wings of an aircraft.
The pavements of a town.		The fields of the farmer.

Only "The wings of an aircraft" offends neither ear nor eye.

2 – The apostrophe used with singular words that end in -s (lass, mistress, boss, stewardess, class) presents few problems:

that lass's temper.	the mistress's hair.	my boss's desk.
my class's mischief-maker.		your stewardess's dress.

3 – Words that add -s for the plural (girls, managers) take the apostrophe after the -s':

a girls' school.	boys' school.	doctors' surgeries.
directors' salaries.	ten managers' jobs.	

4 – Words requiring -es to be added for the plural ought not to produce the mistakes and omissions we see. The correct form:

our bosses' desks.	the hostesses' privileges.
the foxes' lair.	thrushes' nests.

We are not likely to write ***"the old houses' roofs"*** or ***"the dresses' colours"*** but the more fluent **"roofs of the old houses"** and **"colours of the dresses".**

The apostrophe is usually applied to show possession by people and living creatures but often gives way to **of** with things, providing smoother reading and understanding, as shown in the previous paragraph.

A school recognised as one of the best for teaching foreigners in the United Kingdom suggests the apostrophe's use with:

(i) All living creatures and their names, stated or implied *(a horse's mane).*

(ii) Geographical terms *(the world's peoples, the river's reaches, Cromer's sea-front).*

(iii) Expressions of time *(A Midsummer Night's Dream, an hour's journey, a month's salary).*

(iv) A few idioms *(A stone's throw).*

5 – The names Jones, Holmes, Parsons, Meadowes, Fellowes, Richards, Perkins, Burrowes, Potts and others ending with **-s** bring doubts over the apostrophe's use. The answer:

Wrong (but often used)	Corrected
George ***Jones'*** room is never as tidy as Eric ***Hines'***.	George **Jones's** room is never as tidy as Eric **Hines's.**
The club's representative criticised ***Francis'*** style of club management.	The club's representative criticised **Francis's** style of club management.
Newcastle United have played football for many years at ***St. James' Park.***	Newcastle United have played football for many years at **St. James's Park.**

The apostrophe's would-be executioners are invited to consider:

(i) The story of **Mr Jenkin** who had a dispute with his neighbour, a **Mr Jenkins,** over the fence that parts their properties. Ignoring the apostrophe, the executioners will probably write:

Was it Mr Jenkins responsibility to trim the hedge?

Who was responsible? Mr Jenkin or Mr Jenkins? The court decided it was **Mr Jenkin's** fence and, therefore, his responsibility for the trimming, although evidence was given that **Mr Jenkins's son** had been doing it for five years.

(ii) A friend, who is one of the apostrophe's executioners, advised Mr Plummer, who was looking for a house, to inspect number 27 Park Avenue, which was for sale. "I know it is ***Mr Gibbs house***", he said.

Mr Plummer went along to No. 27. At the front door he paused: "Do I ask to see Mr Gibb or Mr Gibbs?" His friend had implied Gibb **(Gibb's house),** but he is one of those "letter-louts" mentioned in the Introduction. A more literate friend would have said "**Mr Gibbs's** house", as the owner is **Mr Gibbs.** The confusion increases in Park Avenue because No. 127 is **Mr Gibb's house.**

Apostrophes clear doubts. The **-'s** identifies Jenkin and Gibbs.

Mistakes or ugly structures with names are common, not only in the simplest writings but in those of the highly-educated.

We sometimes read "Robert ***Burns poems***", and even "Robert ***Burn's poems***", which can mean only "The poems of ***Robert Burn***". It should be either "**Robert Burns's** poems" or a smoother, especially in speech, "The poems of **Robert Burns**".

Pronunciation usually signals the most acceptable construction. We would say **"The Prince of Wales's speech"**, not *"The Prince of Wales' speech"*, and **"That's Mr Tomkins's car"**, not *"Mr Tomkins' car"* (Is he Mr Tomkin or Mr Tomkins?)

6 – In half the examples examined for *Make No Mistake,* the possessive plural for **Jones** was written the "***Jones'*** room". But the plural of Jones is **Joneses,** so we need "**Joneses'** room".

Wrong (but freely used)	Corrected
The ***Burrowes'*** dog next door is called Patch.	The **Burroweses'** dog next door is called Patch.
The ***Meadowes'*** house is in need of immediate repair.	The **Meadoweses'** house is in need of immediate repair.
Can you take the ***Richards'*** children to school today? You are friends of Mr and Mrs Richards, I believe.	Can you take the **Richardses'** children to school today? You are friends of Mr and Mrs Richards, I believe.

7 – When the plural does not end in <u>-s</u> (**woman** becomes **women** and **child** becomes **children**), mistakes are made if the apostrophe is placed after the <u>-s</u>' or omitted altogether, instead of being written before it. Examples:

Wrong	Corrected
Gentlemens privileges in this club are being abused by that ***mans*** behaviour.	**Gentlemen's** privileges in this club are being abused by that **man's** behaviour.
Childrens' toys are too costly for us to give at Christmas this year.	**Children's** toys are too costly for us to give at Christmas this year.
Mens overcoats are on sale at bargain prices in the shop that is closing down.	**Men's** overcoats are on sale at bargain prices in the shop that is closing down.

8 – Omitting both the -s and the apostrophe sometimes reads well without changing meaning or upsetting the grammarian by using a singular noun as an adjective for things. Examples:

Reported (correctly)	Alternatives
The **tractor's** wheelmarks on our roads cause problems.	The **tractor** wheelmarks on our roads cause problems.
The **club's** rules prohibit dogs on the golf course.	The **club** rules prohibit dogs on the golf course.

9 – With some singular words ending in -s, it is customary to add an apostrophe without a further possessive -'s, or to omit the apostrophe altogether. Examples:

for goodness sake. Moses' law. Socrates humour.

To add -'s is said to compel tongue-twisting pronunciation. But what is objectionable in the following, written or spoken?

for goodness's sake. Moses's law. Socrates's humour.

That question was answered by one grammarian the author consulted with: *"Unusual! It's not what we say! Unidiomatic! Un-English!"* Therefore, "for goodness sake" is passed politely here as a colloquialism, though we suggest that it is as difficult to translate into most foreign languages with the right meaning, as are the unsightly English ***awfully nice*** and ***frightfully funny.***

Classical names that end in -s (e.g., Euripedes, Sophocles, Brutus, Archilochus, Alcaeus) are seldom, probably never, seen with the extra -'s. For those of us who wish to retain the general rule for apostrophes the simple alternative is "The plays of Euripedes".

10 – Personal pronouns do not carry an apostrophe. We write:

ours and theirs. his and hers. to its advantage.

It's is short for **it is** or **it has.** Who's is short for **who is** or **who has.** Whose is the possessive of **who,** as in:

Bob Bland, whose bark is worse than his bite, and Bill Hardy, who's a generous man, would willingly help.

NOTE: Avoid ***who's.*** Always write **who is.**

Foreigners ask why the possessive **ours** and other personal pronouns have no apostrophe. They point out that, answering "Whose basket is it?", we write "It's Margaret's", and that no one writes "It's her's". *Make No Mistake* could find no reason. But we are reminded that we do say "One's anger is justified", although it is rarely seen in print.

11 – Names of companies and organisations do not usually display apostrophes. Barclays Bank is never seen nowadays as Barclay's Bank, although that was the universal name many years ago. The title by which any company decides to be known is registered officially, as the law requires for Ltd. or PLC. companies in the United Kingdom.

Smiths Bakery Ltd. and the Kings Crown Hotel Ltd. will be registered as companies. The Tranby Licensed Victuallers Association and the Bookley Stallholders Golf Society will be affiliated to and registered with their chosen official titles on the books of national or local associations.

The POSSESSIVE CASE is also known as the GENITIVE, which means "source, origin or possession". That interpretation raises the question: Is the apostrophe necessary where actual possession is not shown, as in Students Union, Trades Union Congress, sports editor and Highways Agency?

Why not define those titles as compound nouns – a unit of two or more words – and declare the apostrophe to be unnecessary, except, of course, when writing "the Highways Agency's decision…"?

The opinion and practice that the apostrophe has become irrelevant is illustrated in a blatant example from one university in Dr Bernard Lamb's *National Survey of UK Undergraduates' Standards of English.* He reported:

> The student was fairly consistent and punctilious in his punctuation. He is bright, went to normal English schools, and has grade B in GCSE English language and in English literature. He was taught English grammar and punctuation at school, but the apostrophe was never mentioned, so he worked out how to use it from seeing what they did in books.
>
> His essay included: Other metabolic ***disorder's*** have been treated with various ***degree's*** of success…Phenylalinine ***build's*** up in the blood…This ***manifest's*** itself…to treat genetic blood ***disorder's*** by first ***irradicating*** **(eradicating)** a **patient's** stem ***cell's*** and…

The only correct apostrophe is **patient's stem.** All others are wrong. This final-year undergraduate imposed unwanted apostrophes on disorders, degrees, builds, manifests and cells.

SUMMARY – Apostrophes to show possession:

1 – Add apostrophe and an **-s (-'s)** when the word is singular.

The teacher's salary will increase next month.

2 – Place an apostrophe after the **-s (-s')** of a plural word.

The teachers' salaries will increase next month.

3 – Add an apostrophe and an **-s (-'s)** when the plural form of a word does not end in **-s.**

Men's shoes with leather soles have become expensive.

4 – No change of rule when the singular as well as the plural end in **-s.**

The grass's texture becomes the grasses' textures.

Do not write ***Mr Perkins' horse*** or ***the Perkins' horses,*** but **Mr Perkins's horse** and **the Perkinses' horses.**

5 – Personal pronouns **(ours, hers,** etc.) take no apostrophe, except **one's.**

Inconsistent use of the apostrophe and, too often, ignorance of its purpose, make powerful arguments in support of an English Language Authority, proposed by Geoffrey Kitchin in *The Last Word (pages 178, 179)* and supported unreservedly by the author of *Make No Mistake.* As there are doubts about the apostrophe's place in so many minds, recommendations would be well received, except by those for whom anything is acceptable.

Reference to the literature of the Middle English period (1000-1500) shows **-es** as indication of possession. Examples:

We both be at our wittes end – *John Heywood* (1497-1580).

A mery someres day – *Chaucer* (1340-1400).

Footmens' outfits a cut above the rest

Principle Public Relations Officer

Salary up to £25,437 p.a.

Home Secretaries' son

meets the most recent incumbent in Sir Francis Drakes's old home

Prove it's democratic nature by allowing any of it's members who wish to leave

Society plague to Sir Winston

A PLAGUE to commemorate the late Sir Winston Churchill's four-year stay in Epping is planned

of a high order.
He or she's responsibilities will include the effective co-ordination of

An Englishmans' home

Footmen's outfits a cut above the rest

Principal Public Relations Officer

Salary up to £25,437 p.a.

meets the most recent incumbent in Sir Francis Drake's old home

Home Secretary's son

Prove its democratic nature by allowing any of its members who wish to leave

Society plaque to Sir Winston

A PLAQUE to commemorate the late Sir Winston Churchill's four-year stay in Epping is planned

of a high order.
His or her responsibilities will include the effective co-ordination of

An Englishman's home

Punctuation

Write it as you speak it

Punctuation is important, sometimes essential, to meaning. Many writers, not only school-leavers but senior managers as well, omit a lot of commas and full stops in letters, memoranda and reports, as if words alone were sufficient. They write, or approve with a signature, business and private messages that could be likened to a speech pitched on one note without a pause.

The example that follows is taken from a letter that made sense when the sender dictated it but had to be read twice by the receiver to be understood. Helpful commas and a full stop are missing.

LETTER – improperly punctuated

The company having collapsed the building could not be completed which meant that the couple who had spent their savings on a deposit were almost destitute, however help has been promised.

PUNCTUATED – properly

The company having collapsed, the building could not be completed, which meant that the couple, who had spent their savings on a deposit, were almost destitute. However, help has been promised.

The full stop omitted after the word **admittance** in part of a letter *(below)* from a gas company is another example of managerial failure to punctuate properly:

> Our inspector called yesterday to make a special reading of your meter but was unable to gain admittance if you return the card he left a new appointment can be arranged.

Commas smooth the reading of everything in print or script; as would one after the word **left** *(above)*. Some editors and writers have dismissed them as ugly typographical interruptions. That opinion is rejected here. Commas are as necessary in text as are signposts in the countryside.

Sentences in newspapers and magazines a hundred years ago were much longer than is usual today, with many more commas and semi-colons. Some publications now encourage authors of articles and reporters to limit them to 20-25 words, using the minimum of commas.

Short sentences, however, irritate some readers with prose that is stilted – they become a catalogue of facts – but one must accept that those of six words or fewer are understood at a glance. A child of six wrote this example:

> Our car has broken down. It is ten years old. It is rusty.

At the end of each of the three sentences, a speaker's voice drops and pauses, indicating a full stop. Each begins with a capital letter. Each has a subject **(Our car)** and each has a predicate **(has broken down).** Linked into one sentence, with commas instead of full stops, the jerk is taken out of reading:

> Our car, which is ten years old and rusty, has broken down.

Commas mark the two shorter pauses, with voice at the same level. Both stops mark change of thought or introduce extra information.

In longer passages, where a speaker would pause not merely to take breath but to convey the meaning clearly, punctuation is required. A missing comma often compels one to read a sentence a second or third time to understand it. Any check in the voice indicates probable need of a comma or full stop if the words are to be written; occasionally a semi-colon or colon may be preferred. Consider, therefore, this simple prescription for punctuating:

> **Use the pauses that come naturally in speech to punctuate the words you write.**

Test that recommendation by selecting a paragraph with sentences of 20 words or more from a newspaper or magazine and ask someone to read it aloud at first sight. The voice is certain to tell you if the necessary commas and full stops are there. The speaker's natural pauses will identify them. If they have been left out, he or she will stumble through the text. The confusion that dashes commonly create, when they enclose more than half-a-dozen words, will also be heard.

The pause-then-punctuate practice, if followed, should ensure that all well-constructed sentences and paragraphs are understood at a glance. But the pause theory is an aid, not a rule. No comma is needed in longer sentences when the words are already passing smoothly before a reader's eyes, even if a speaker at some point would break momentarily for breath. An example from an insurance policy:

> Insurance provides for the loan of a replacement appliance free of charge in the event of our service engineers being unable to repair your appliance in your home.

When to use
The FULL STOP

A full stop marks the end of a sentence, which is a group of words that are complete grammatically:

The sun is shining. We shall swim in the lake.

The two can be linked by **and** to make one sentence.

A common and increasing failure is to string together several sentences with commas instead of breaking them up with full stops. In many private letters, full stops are neglected, and placed only at the end of paragraphs. Example:

LETTER – improperly punctuated

The football season has just about finished, there are two games still to be played, we shall watch one tonight.

PUNCTUATED – properly

The football season has just about finished. There are two games still to be played. ***We shall watch one tonight.

***__And__ *could link two sentences, probably preceded by a comma because there is a change of subject.*

Full stops are not added to questions – Who is there? – or to exclamations – Hurrah!

ABBREVIATIONS have lost most punctuation marks in modern usage, as in USA, BBC, BSc, NATO, MP, UNESCO, DSO.

A capital letter begins a sentence and a full stop ends one. But doubts appear over the full stop's placement with quotation marks. Should it be inside or outside? The author prefers:

The demonstrators shouted "We want more money".	►	Full stop OUTSIDE because it completes a whole sentence.
"She cried in agony until someone rescued her."	►	Full stop INSIDE because whole sentence is within a quotation.
He said: "The crowd sang 'God save the Queen' before the football match started".	►	Full stop OUTSIDE because it marks end of sentence that begins with "He said".
	►	But most people place full stop INSIDE ("...started.")

The COMMA

The comma is the shortest stop, most frequently used and most frequently wrongly used or omitted. Its purposes are summarised under seven headings:

(1) When places, things or descriptive words are listed:

He visited Paris, Belgrade, Rome and Barcelona.

My secretary is highly competent, personable, ambitious, and much involved in the company's social activities.

(2) Before and after clauses introduced by **who, which** or **whose,** where the subject is already clearly identified and the clause merely supplies extra information.

The managing director, who joined the company three months ago, has been dismissed.

(3) Before and after words and phrases such as **therefore, nevertheless, of course, however** and **in my opinion** when placed within a sentence:

It is likely, nevertheless, that he will be dismissed.

(4) Commas may enclose a phrase which provides additional information about a subject, even without **who** or **which:**

Birmingham, the second largest city in England, hopes one day to host the Olympic Games.

(5) Although **and** and **but** usually connect two sections of a sentence without a comma, one may be needed if there is a clear change of subject, or the length of its first section requires a natural pause when read aloud, as in:

The eloquence of an orator may hold listeners spellbound at a public meeting, but the influence cannot be compared to the effects of the same face and voice on the television screen.

(6) When a sentence begins with a subordinate clause or phrase, a comma is needed before the main clause. *(For definition of subordinate clauses and phrases see The Combination that makes a Sentence, pages 19-21).* Example:

Before you catch the train to Newcastle, spare me a few minutes for a private chat.

If George visits London next week, he will try to meet you.

Although the sea was cold, we swam every day.

(7) When a place, person or object is described with emphasis, the pause we make in speech indicates the need of a comma after extra adjectives. This description would probably be snapped off the tongue like the crack of a whip:

He is a wicked, quarrelsome, selfish, old man.

In the following two sentences, there is no pause, so no commas are needed in describing the employer or lad:

Our generous old employer died. He was a clever little man.

Using Commas for clarity

A missing comma seldom changes the meaning to intelligent readers, but its omission can frustrate them. Eyes have to turn back to understand a phrase or sentence – or, more likely, the whole paragraph will be abandoned.

<table>
<tr><th>Wrong</th><th>Corrected</th></tr>
<tr><td>The cars having passed the bus turned sharply into West Street.</td><td>The cars |,| having passed |,| the bus turned sharply into West Street.</td></tr>
<tr><td></td><td>OR The cars |,| having passed the bus |,| turned sharply into West Street.</td></tr>
<tr><td>The storm over the hill became a magnificent sight as the sun went down.</td><td>The storm over |,| the hill became a magnificent sight as the sun went down.</td></tr>
<tr><td>In the rooms above the tenants behaved noisily.</td><td>In the rooms above |,| the tenants behaved noisily.</td></tr>
<tr><td>The prisoner said the judge was unscrupulous and a menace to society.</td><td>The prisoner |,| said the judge |,| was unscrupulous and a menace to society.</td></tr>
<tr><td>The young thief drove the car as far as I could see into the River Tamar near the bridge.</td><td>The young thief drove the car |,| as far as I could see |,| into the River Tamar near the bridge.</td></tr>
<tr><td>If hungry foxes can run through my garden to find my neighbour's chickens.</td><td>If hungry |,| foxes can run through my garden to find my neighbour's chickens.</td></tr>
</table>

When punctuating with commas changes the meaning

A – (i) All the firm's engineers who went to Mauritius last year will miss the firm's trip to Italy this year.

Meaning – SOME of the firm's engineers went to Mauritius last year. Others will go to Italy this year.

(ii) ALL the firm's engineers |,| who went to Mauritius last year |,| will miss the trip to Italy this year.

Meaning – NO engineers will go to Italy this year.

B – (i) The boys who disliked playing tennis took up athletics.

Meaning – SOME of the boys disliked playing tennis.

(ii) The boys |,| who disliked playing tennis |,| took up athletics.

Meaning – ALL the boys disliked playing tennis.

C – (i) The grapes which have been harvested were sold today.

Meaning – SOME of the grapes have been harvested.

(ii) The grapes |,| which have been harvested |,| were sold today.

Meaning – ALL the grapes have been harvested.

D – (i) My father is in favour of banning all insecticides which can affect wild life.

Meaning – He would ban only insecticides that can affect wild life.

(ii) My father is in favour of banning all insecticides |,| which can affect wild life.

Meaning – He would ban all insecticides. It is the writer's comment that they can affect wild life.

E – (i) For members at the opening ceremony only |,| seats in the two front rows will be available.

Meaning – Seats available in two front rows for members, but only at the opening ceremony.

(ii) For members at the opening ceremony |,| only seats in the two front rows will be available.

Meaning – They are the only seats available for members at the opening ceremony.

The SEMI-COLON

The semi-colon is now to the English language what the steam engine is to the railway (remember that steam engines are still to be seen in some parts of the country).

(1) Search your newspaper; in a downmarket tabloid few semi-colons are likely to be seen, except in lists of details.

(2) Look at the *Oxford Dictionary of Quotations* to see how writers of the past used semi-colons dozens of times, as examples (a) and (b) below show:

(a) I swear she's no chicken; she's on the wrong side of thirty, if she be a day. – *Jonathan Swift*

(b) Claret is the liquor for boys; port for men; but he who aspires to be a hero must drink brandy. – *Samuel Johnson*

The semi-colon marks a longer pause than a comma and comes at the end of a complete statement, as illustrated in (1), (a) and (b) above. In (1), a full stop could replace the semi-colon; not a comma. In (a), a full stop is also the alternative. In (b), commas would suffice.

The second statements after semi-colons in (1) and (a) are closely related to the first and are a natural follow-on. A full stop, while readily understood and acceptable, would make an abrupt change.

In speech, the semi-colon, full stop and dash do not exist, but pauses suggest or determine their use in writing. A secretary taking dictation probably transcribes the longer pauses into full stops or dashes, although a semi-colon is often apt. Punctuation is not a rigid discipline. The full stop, semi-colon or dash could be used in the following:

How to find the money for this week's wages is a frightening problem (; . or –) the bank has closed the company's credit.

The islands are vulnerable to hurricanes (; . or –) already insurance companies require huge premiums.

At home, he was the kindest and most considerate parent anyone would wish to meet (; . or –) at work, most of his staff thought he was a tyrant.

Will the semi-colon return to favour? Does it contribute to style? Now that the anything-will-do-as-long-as-it-is-understood attitude is viewed with contempt officially, with demands for a keener edge to English-language teaching it may reappear in numbers. It offers an alternative structure to a sequence of short, jerky sentences, which may provide clarity but has the reader jumping over the full stops as if they were hurdles. Weigh that argument with the following example *(not necessarily commended)* taken from a magazine:

> Later, with the sun shining, they went to the beach; swimming was a craze among the whole party; and, in the evening, they sat down to a barbecue meal on the lawn.

Common use of the semi-colon is to separate details in a list similar to this one:

> We send you names and addresses of the three witnesses: Mr James Bradlough, 176 Brand Street, Pilcaster; Mrs Ethel Mouncer, The Lawns, Clumpit Hill, Cremerton; and Miss Joan Bickleton, 5 Sten Close, Bammington.

The COLON

The colon was once in constant use to mark a longer pause than any stop except the full stop. But its original purpose, to separate a double sentence, has almost disappeared. It is retained mainly in two forms:

1 – To introduce a list of names, places or things.

> The travel agency is expanding, with holidays next year in the following countries: Thailand, Cyprus, Hungary, Finland, Egypt, South Africa, Peru and China.

2 – To introduce a quotation or statement, usually longer than five or six words.

> Mr Smith said: "Theft of stock in this store has turned profit into a big loss and we may have to close down".

The colon is used freely in these pages to introduce details, a cause or a result (Example above – *It is retained mainly in two forms:...*). It occasionally separates double sentences in the leading articles of newspapers. Examples:

> This practice ought to be prevented: guardians of law and order who murder people are subverting the very thing they are supposed to uphold.

> Unilateral disarmament has moral attractions: it is arguably wrong to have weapons which, if used, would kill so many people so indiscriminately.

Without detracting from those colons, semi-colons or full stops would serve the same purpose.

The DASH

Dashes punctuate (a) in pairs before and after a phrase in the middle of a sentence, and (b) before adding a fact or an explanation at the end of a sentence. Examples:

(a) They were a band of mercenaries – some of them former policemen – who had been persuaded to join the expedition for large sums of money.

(b) The headmaster wants twenty boys to apply for places at universities – that would be a record for the school.

Those examples are acceptable, although in (a) commas would be satisfactory, and in (b) a full stop, colon or semi-colon would ensure equal understanding.

Dashes have become an obsession with many writers, to the point that the interruption they create in the middle of a sentence often shunts frustrated readers away from an article. By the time the words between the dashes have been read, the start of the sentence has been forgotten. Example:

Dressed in a two-piece suit with a red waistcoat – never underestimate the element of nostalgia in a man's wardrobe, even if the gold watch and chain were missing this time – Arnold Smith went to a party that was certain to renew many old acquaintances.

That is a simplified version of a sentence in a London newspaper. Between the dashes, the writer has introduced an afterthought. It should have been broken into two sentences.

A break of more than three of four words can disturb the reader's comprehension. Resorting to **which** or **who** between commas often provides easier reading, as below.

Reported	**Preferred**
The King's Head inn, – it has been in the market place at East Dudham since the reign of George the Fourth and is a Grade 1 listed building – closes tomorrow when Ted Elder retires.	The King's Head inn, which has been in the market place at East Dudham since the reign of George the Fourth, closes tomorrow, when Ted Elder retires. It is a Grade 1 listed building.

Afterthoughts between dashes are seldom seen in letters; they are a development mainly in newspapers.

The dash is sometimes used to give emphasis or dramatic impact to a statement:

> Although Sally has put her name down for next week's shorthand examination, she trembles at the thought of one depressing fact – that she has failed four times already.
>
> They searched for a day and all night until they found him in the dyke – murdered.

Whenever a dash is written, a degree of suddenness or change of thought is imparted. The same interpolation when spoken is better understood because the voice can inflect meaning.

BRACKETS

Brackets have almost disappeared from narrative writing but are widely retained to break up detail more effectively than commas and semi-colons, as seen in the following comparison:

Reported	Preferred
Members of the society's new executive committee are: Alfred Jessup, Wroxham; James Ake, Dundee; Tim Beswetherick, Keynsham; George Fish, Kirk Langley.	Members of the society's new executive committee are: Alfred Jessup (Wroxham), James Ake (Dundee), Tim Beswetherick (Keynsham), George Fish (Kirk Langley).

Dashes are written instead of brackets, perhaps too often, in letters, reports, essays and memoranda. They interrupt the flow abruptly, whereas brackets allow the eye to pass more freely over the text. Brackets are preferred to dashes or commas in the following:

> The first Earl of Stockton (as Harold Macmillan, Conservative Prime Minister, 1957-63) became Chancellor of Oxford University in 1960.

Most of the afterthoughts or explanatory phrases within brackets, however, could be placed between two dashes or two commas. The additional information in the example below would be more appropriately placed inside commas than brackets:

> Peter Smithson (the well-known broadcaster) will perform the opening ceremony.

MEMORANDA: mistakes and omissions

Reading documents, articles, letters and newspaper reports is easier when punctuation is intelligently used, apostrophes are in place and the spelling is accurate. That is commonsense.

Write it as you speak it, which this book commends, is a sensible guide for the placement of full stops and commas. The apostrophe has a strong grammatical base and can affect meaning as well as instant understanding. Use of a dictionary should prevent problems with spelling.

A group of young women co-operated with the author in an exercise at the start of their one-year secretarial course. The object was to explore areas of their language that needed revision and to confirm the original idea for *Make No Mistake.* All possessed A-level or equivalent qualifications.

The two hours spent in discussion, starting with a dictated test, showed the priorities to be: (1) Punctuation, (2) use of the apostrophe and (3) spelling.

The fact that spelling produced most mistakes was not particularly important because dictionaries were not at hand. The speaker explained fully his punctuate-at-the-pauses' practice but he could not apply it himself at the time

THE TEXT, as dictated

From: Chief Executive **MEMORANDUM**

To: Head of Sales

Your department was committed last January to a much lower budget in the promotion of sales. That commitment has not been fulfilled. Salesmen's expenses have broken all records and, at the board's request, an immediate cut of 15 per cent has to be made. I had recommended 20 per cent, because staff are using four-star hotel accommodation when three-star would be adequate. Further, £20-a-head lunches are being charged to entertain people who, nine times out of ten, place orders for little or nothing.

One salesman, as you know, was dismissed when you were on holiday. He picked up another man's bill for £40 at a restaurant and submitted it with his expenses' sheet. He had called only to buy a sandwich and a lager at the bar.

The managing director's note to me says our company's selling costs have soared and the Chairman said yesterday, "Be ruthless or there must be redundancies".

because he had to dictate slowly. Sadly, in transcription, the idea had not been understood or it was ignored, and the papers handed in suggested that the students' earlier education had given the minimum attention to punctuation, the apostrophe and spelling.

Not one transcript would have been passed for distribution in any well-run office without careful editing. All had blind spots with the apostrophe. That is not surprising because, in many advertisements and business communications, the apostrophe is neglected. "The farm's animals" or "The farms' animals" become "The farms animals". One farm or more? And televised and newspaper advertisements illustrate contempt for the apostrophe every day.

The failure to punctuate properly and disregard of the apostrophe are seen in one trainee-secretary's transcript *(spelling mistakes have been corrected)*. The apostrophe, as far as her education was concerned, did not exist and, in punctuation, the comma was the equivalent of a full stop.

Compare that transcript with the original text. Be advised, however, that at the end of the course few of the deficiencies seen here remained, such was the quality of the tutor. She insisted on taking the dictation herself with the students and handed in a paper that was a hundred per cent accurate.

TRANSCRIPT – An example to be compared with text dictated

From: Chief Executive **MEMORANDUM**

To: Head of Sales

Your department was committed last January to a much lower budget in the promotion of sales, that commitment has not been fulfilled. Salesmens expenses have broken all records and at the boards request an immediate cut of 15% has to be made, I had recommended 20% because staff are using Four Star Hotel accommodation when Three Star would be adequate, further £20-a-head lunches are being charged to entertain people who nine times out of ten place orders for little or nothing.

One salesman as you know was dismissed when you were on holiday, he picked up another man's bill for £40 at a restaurant and submitted it with his expenses sheet, he had called only to buy a sandwich and a beer at the bar.

The managing directors note to me says our companys selling costs have soared and the Chairman said yesterday be ruthless or there must be redundancies.

BUSINESS LETTER (unacceptable)

Elementary mistakes appear not only in family letters and school homework. Managers at the higher levels of business and the professions who dictate into audio machines or to shorthand writers sometimes sign the resultant typescript without recognising errors. The responsibility to dispatch a faultless document is with them, not with their secretaries. Punctuation, apostrophes, paragraphs and even spelling should be clarified during dictation if mistakes are likely.

An example of the English sent out from some corners of the business world is seen in a letter from the branch manager of a large national distribution agency. The principal paragraph, which concerns a missing package, is reprinted, not to pillory the unnamed manager but to show that errors in grammar, style and clarity persist, despite education at a level expected to provide supervisors in industry.

THE LETTER (extract)

The employee responsible for handing out undelivered parcels to callers, said that checking the parcels for which forms notifieing attempted delivery, for those which had been held for more than 21 days, any found on hand after this period of time are treated as undelivered and returned to sender, he found one for .... Hill which had not been endorsed to the effect that the form about undelivered parcels had been left, he therefore put this parcel back in the appropriate delivery container for a further attempt to be made to deliver it or for it to be correctly endorsed. As the parcel was not returned properly endorsed to the callers container, it was considered that it had been delivered.

The manager, who controlled a staff of about 40, said later that he was without secretarial help at the time he wrote it.

RE-WRITTEN

The employee responsible for handing out undelivered parcels to callers said that, on checking, he found one for .... Hill. It was not endorsed to show that a form had been left at the address to notify the householder that delivery had been attempted. He put the parcel back in the appropriate container, and he expected it would be correctly endorsed if the next delivery attempt failed. As the parcel was not subsequently returned to the caller's bin, he believed it had been delivered. Parcels held for more than 21 days are treated as undelivered and returned to the sender.

DICTATION (with perfection in mind)

Everyone who dictates letters or reports to someone with a notebook or into an audio recorder, has a personal style, ranging from "I leave it to you to get it right for me" to the punctilious dictator who clears the doubts when spoken.

Some writers – many of them secretaries – have a better knowledge of English than those who dictate and can be expected to transcribe speech into acceptable language. But most good typescripts are the result of co-operative effort.

An educated person will see the punctuation, paragraphing, apostrophes and spelling problems in his or her mind's eye when speaking and will identify them. Accuracy and mutual satisfaction follow, as in this example which has the spoken clarifications bracketed in italics:

> Dear Mr Jones,
>
> Thank you for your letter of yesterday's date *(Stop)*. I regret that you do not explain the failure to deliver the goods to our Hayle depot *(Hayle is* **H** *for Hotel,* **A** *for Alpha,* **Y** *for Yankee,* **L** *for Lima,* **E** *for Echo,* **H A Y L E***)* until today *(Stop, paragraph)*.
>
> Your Mr Hardy *(that's Hardy with a* **Y***)* had assured me that there would be no delay *(Stop)*. The result has been considerable loss of business for three days this week and we shall expect at least an extra discount *(Comma)*, of say 2½ per cent *(Comma)*, as part compensation *(Stop, paragraph)*.
>
> My company's long association with you *(Comma)*, and your father before you *(Comma)*, allows no thought of another supplier *(Comma)*, although we face constant salesmanship from other sources *(Stop)*. Parkin's *(apostrophe* **s***)* factory is one *(stop, paragraph)*.
>
> This letter gives me an opportunity to invite you and Tom Phillips (that is Phillips with two **Ls***)* to our annual golf meeting at Lyme Regis on July 15th *(Stop)*.
>
> Yours sincerely,

So little attention is given to the possessive apostrophe in many sectors of modern education that clarification is often necessary when business letters are dictated. Mistakes, especially illiteracy, impair reputations. A well-known mail order company sent out beautifully illustrated leaflets advertising ***mens' shirts*** and other articles of clothing. Another company persisted with ***Childrens' shoes*** in large type in national newspaper advertisements.

Punctuation and the apostrophe expose the most common mistakes in virtually all written English. Examples taken from business correspondence, further education classrooms, advertising brochures, the printed media and private postbags bear witness to that statement.

Wrong	Corrected
The ***worlds*** largest cruise liner left Southampton an hour after ***yesterdays*** high tide.	The **world's** largest cruise liner left Southampton an hour after **yesterday's** high tide.
Todays budget speech puts very little extra into any ***workers'*** pay packet, the Chancellor regretted being unable to reduce taxes.	**Today's** budget speech puts very little extra into any **worker's** pay packet. The Chancellor regretted being unable to reduce taxes.
Its my ***son's-in-law*** house, that needs a new roof not my ***brothers.***	**It's** my **son-in-law's** house that needs a new roof, not my **brother's.**
Those books are my ***fathers.***	Those books are my **father's.**
The ***lawyers*** opinion is that ***Smiths*** demands are beyond the ***Jones'*** resources, the ***mans*** nasty attitude makes friendly agreement unlikely, ***the courts*** ruling is needed. Our worry is the ***childrens*** future, where will they be living in a ***years*** time?	The **lawyer's** opinion is that **Smith's** demands are beyond the **Joneses'** resources. The **man's** nasty attitude makes friendly agreement unlikely. **The court's** ruling is needed. Our worry is the **children's** future. Where will they be living in a **year's** time?
Heddons Mouth is one of the most rewarding of the ***National Trusts*** properties in Devon, it is one of the least known.	**Heddon's Mouth** is one of the most rewarding of the **National Trust's** properties in Devon. It is one of the least known.
I shall not confide again in ***a man, who*** immediately passes on the information to one of my competitors.	I shall not confide again in **a man who** immediately passes on the information to one of my competitors.
Help!. Is no one there?.	Help! Is no one there?
You will of course have to pay an entrance fee.	You will |,| of course |,| have to pay an entrance fee.

A letter to the Editor of the *Daily Telegraph,* London, in February, 1993, is reprinted with the permission of its author, Professor D.M. Davies. It followed an A-level examiner's report that revealed serious English language weaknesses in the papers of many 18-year-old students.

Dear Sir,

The deplorable standard of English observed by A-level examiners cannot be blamed entirely on teachers. Some of our public institutions are helping to destroy our language, at least as far as punctuation is concerned.

The rot set in many years ago when some major banks, such as Barclays and Lloyds, omitted the apostrophe (Barclay's, Lloyd's) from their names.

They have been joined by many large shops, which have abandoned the apostrophe not only in their names but also in their department signs (womens, mens); and by municipal authorities who rarely include a necessary apostrophe in street names (St Andrews Place, Regents Park). Health service hospitals, too, are prime offenders in this respect (Childrens Ward).

It is difficult to discover whether these omissions are the fault of lazy or illiterate signwriters or of incompetent or illiterate managers; but, sadly, few people seem to care.

Prof. D.M. DAVIES
Boston Spa,
West Yorkshire.

Quotation Marks

The choice: Single '....' or Double "...."

Quotation marks, represented by inverted commas, are used mainly to begin and end (a) statements taken from other sources, and (b) words that are slang or written with an unnatural meaning. Examples:

(a) It was Nelson's signal at Trafalgar: "England expects every man to do his duty".

He is another victim of "the slings and arrows of outrageous fortune".

(b) The fighting has already been "shot", and the film should be ready for the cinema next year.

The old man is a "rum" character.

Quotation marks can be applied with double or single inverted commas, according to a publisher's or writer's preference:

1 – **Double** inverted commas.

The protestors ran along the city's main streets waving banners and shouting "We want work".

A second pair of quotation marks, using single inverted commas, is needed inside the first pair if there is a second quotation. Example:

The union's president said: "This is a critical time for all our members and I am sure the cries of those protestors, 'We want work', will be heeded".

Erratum: protesters, not *protestors (old English)*

An expression such as a "cool card", written to describe a person, probably requires inverted commas.

2 – **Single** inverted commas.

The cashier replied to every question about the missing cash with a categorical, 'I have taken nothing'.

Double inverted commas will be required inside the singles:

The manager telephoned his employer to tell him: 'The cashier says repeatedly "I have taken nothing" and I believe him'.

Slang: Most of them were "pickled" (intoxicated).

Wrong	Corrected
Mr Smith said: "It was disgraceful of you to say to Brenda ***"You are a thief"*** without checking the stock again".	Mr Smith said: "It was disgraceful of you to say to Brenda **'You are a thief'** without checking the stock again".

Punctuation in sentences with quotation marks is another personal choice. There is no accepted authority. Four English language professors were asked for a ruling and they, in effect, said: "Leave it to the printer"!

The examples above have commas and full stops outside both single and double inverted commas. But the argument to place them inside is equally strong. The only advice here is: Make a decision and keep to it.

The author has chosen in this book to place the full stop inside the final quotation mark when the whole sentence is inside quotation marks ("   .") and outside when the quoted passage is part of a sentence (.........."   ".).

Punctuation in front of a quotation is also a personal choice. When it is short, many writers prefer either a comma or no mark. When it is eight words or more, the colon is normally favoured. She shouted "Stop it!" Mr Jaffa said: "It is time we did something about that pollution, or there will be an outbreak of dysentery".

Long quotations: When a quotation runs to more than one paragraph, the marks should be placed at the beginning of each paragraph and only at the end of the last one. Example:

> Mr Smith said: "It will be a long time before this company recovers from the strike, which lasted nine weeks and cost 16 million in lost production. *(No inverted commas here)*
>
> "However, that's all behind us and, unless our competitors have taken away most of our customers permanently, the banks are unlikely to bankrupt us".

Books, plays and films are wrapped in single or double quotation marks ("David Copperfield", 'Bitter Lemons') or printed in italics *(David Copperfield, Bitter Lemons).*

Learning by Example

COMMON MISTAKES

Part one – A and B

1 – A, An and The

Pronunciation determines use of **a** or **an.** The general rule is that **a** is placed before all words starting with a consonant sound (a bottle, a cat, a door, a woman) and **an** before those starting with a vowel sound (an apple, an eagle, an illness).

An replaces *a* before words which start with a silent **h** (i.e., they start with a vowel sound). Examples: **an** heir, **an** honour.

A replaces *an* before consonant sounds even if the first letters are vowels: **a** unique, **a** unit, **a** union, **a** eulogy.

Wrong	Corrected
The club's chairman cannot expect *an unanimous* vote about a new building.	The club's chairman cannot expect **a unanimous** vote about a new building.
Stormy weather means that they will be *a hour* late.	Stormy weather means that they will be **an hour** late.

2 – When A/An or The are wrongly omitted

Omission of **the** or **a/an** can change meanings. "The **young elms and oaks** are free of disease" implies that both elms and oaks are young. But only the elms are young, so we write "The **young elms and the oaks** are free of disease".

Ambiguous or Wrong	Intended
A salesman and experienced lorry driver wanted for a fruit farm – Apply....	A salesman and **an** experienced lorry driver wanted for a fruit farm – Apply....
• *One person wanted*	• *Two to be employed*
They will be seeing the chairman and chief executive tomorrow.	They will be seeing the chairman and **the** chief executive tomorrow.
• *Seeing one person*	• *Seeing two*
During one week last month, an avalanche and rainstorm wrought havoc.	During one week last month, an avalanche and **a** rainstorm wrought havoc.
• *Avalanche and rain together*	• *Two separate events*

3 – About

About has become one of the most used words in the English language. When it means concerning, relative to, we read: "I want to talk to you **about** the financial crisis at tomorrow's meeting. That is what the meeting is all **about**".

When the definition is approximately, around, we read: "He will be here **about** seven o'clock". Superfluous words are often added, resulting in poor English *(see examples below)*.

Reported	Corrected
The headmaster hopes to send reports to parents next week, ***about the 9th or 10th*** of May.	The headmaster hopes to send reports to parents next week, **on the 9th or 10th** of May.
We must buy ***about two or three*** new chairs for the dining room.	We must buy **two or three** new chairs for the dining room.

4 – Adjectives that should not be compared

Anything **full** cannot be *fuller*. One jug cannot be the *fullest* of ten. Definition of **full:** Having no vacant space, containing all that can or should be admitted.

Speakers and writers take licence with *fuller* and *fullest* to mark emphasis, but it is a distortion, as seen and heard in the use of many other adjectives that are absolutes.

Adjective	Wrong
full	*fuller, fullest*
empty	*emptier, emptiest*
complete	*completest or most complete*
perfect	*more or most perfect*
absolute	*more or most absolute*
matchless	*more or most matchless*
fatal	*more or most fatal*
worthless	*more or most worthless*
wooden	*more or most wooden*
impossible	*more or most impossible*
unique	*more or most unique*
superlative	*more or most superlative*
universal	*more or most universal*
unanimous	*more or most unanimous*
supreme	*more or most supreme*
total	*more or most total*

5 – Adjectives – wrong use of More and Most

A mistake occasionally heard, although rarely written, is use of **more** and **most** in front of comparatives and superlatives. People in high places have been known to commit this grammatical heresy, probably through haste when speaking without a script. Two examples *(below)* heard on radio, the first *(more harder)* in the speech of a well-known politician:

Wrong	Corrected
You will find it *more harder* to climb that mountain than the hills near your home.	You will find it **harder** to climb that mountain than the hills near your home.
He is the *most funniest* man this town has ever seen on the stage.	He is the **funniest** man this town has ever seen on the stage.

6 – Adopt or Adapt?

To adapt is to adjust to a new situation, to reconstruct an appliance for a different or additional purpose (changing the rear of a car to pull a trailer); to comply with new regulations set by an organisation; to bring about and accept a change in one's way of life (e.g., after inheriting a fortune).

To adopt is to accept another person's suggestion or to bring up a child who is not your own (in most countries that is usually a boy or girl adopted with legal consent).

Wrong	Corrected
Fred will quickly *adopt himself* to the electronic tools he will have to use in his new job.	Fred will quickly **adapt himself** to the electronic tools he will have to use in his new job.
Primrose and the other girls in the hotel's kitchens *must adapt* the new strict rules about hygiene, or go.	Primrose and the other girls in the hotel's kitchens **must adopt** the new strict rules about hygiene, or go.

7 – Advice or Advise?

Advice *(noun)* is an opinion or recommendation to help another person to decide about action to be taken, or a job to be done.

Advise is the verb – **to advise.** "Your brother **was advised** by his family to take his **doctor's advice.** He must lose weight." It is often used in business instead of announce or tell – **"Advise us** when we can expect the next coach from Glasgow".

Wrong	Corrected
My lawyer's *advise* is to claim all the money those customers owe the company.	My lawyer's **advice** is to claim all the money those customers owe the company.
They adviced sowing seeds in April and it proved to be good *advise.*	**They advised** sowing seeds in April and it proved to be good **advice.**
I am adviced that your contract implies a heavy penalty for late completion.	**I am advised** that your contract implies a heavy penalty for late completion.

8 – Affect or Effect

To affect *(verb)* means to influence or to change a thing, person or circumstances. "Poor ventilation **affects working conditions** in a factory." The word is never a noun.

To effect *(verb)* means to bring about or to achieve something. "The treatment **effected a big improvement** in the patient's condition."

The effect *(noun)* or **an effect** means the result of an action or influence. "My advice seemed to have **no effect** whatever."

Wrong	Corrected
The £40,000 she won will not ***effect*** her lifestyle.	The £40,000 she won will not **affect** her lifestyle.
Oil effects the soil.	**Oil affects** the soil.
The affect of the riots was to close down our business.	**The effect** of the riots was to close down our business.

9 – Agree with or Agree to?

The difference is clear but mistakes are frequent. Test for error by speaking the sentence before writing it.

Agree to = Consent to. Examples make plain the use. **"I agree to pay** you £1000 for the gold bracelet, and **I agree to go** with you to Worcester next week."

Agree with = Approve of, share an opinion. Example: **"I agree with you** that £1000 is a fair price for the bracelet, and **I agree with** your idea about the visit to Worcester next week".

Wrong	Corrected
I agree with writing you an article for your magazine.	**I agree to** write an article for your magazine.
Tom agrees to you when you try to persuade the family to move to another area.	**Tom agrees with** you when you try to persuade the family to move to another area.

NOTE: We can also **agree about** (a subject) and we can **agree on** the date and place of our next meeting.

10 – Agreement – singular verbs with singular subjects

A singular verb **(is)** partners a singular subject **(man).** A plural verb **(are)** goes with a plural subject **(men).** When **and** links two subjects (a tiger and an elephant) the verb is plural, with rare exceptions. It is natural to say "Cheese and biscuits **is** also on the menu", since the two units of food are regarded as one. (Hyphenate cheese-and-biscuits).

Agreement (numbers)

Wrong	Corrected
Wind and rain ruins any summer holiday in the United Kingdom.	**Wind and rain ruin** any summer holiday in the United Kingdom.
The *sight* of the mountains *were* the most memorable of a holiday in Switzerland.	The **sight** of the mountains **was** the most memorable of a holiday in Switzerland.

Agreement (persons)

Wrong	Corrected
Every headmaster wants the best examination results even if *their* pupils have a bad record for truancy.	**Every headmaster** wants the best examination results even if **his** pupils have a bad record for truancy.
Boxers have a strict medical examination before *he* enters the ring.	**Boxers** have a strict medical examination before **they** enter the ring.

When AND links two subjects

Wrong	Corrected
The chairman of the company and his daughter *was* there.	The chairman of the company and his daughter **were** there.
	The chairman, with his daughter, **was** there.

11 – All ready or Already?

Confusion exists but the meanings are wide. **All ready** tells us that everybody or everything is here or there for the purpose required. **Already** = Before now, by now, even now, even then.

Wrong	Corrected
They are *already to go* to the union meeting and then to meet the chairman and the managing director.	They are **all ready to go** to the union meeting and then to meet the chairman and the managing director.
All ready they have spent most of their holiday money, with still three days of the holiday left!	**Already** they have spent most of their holiday money, with still three days of the holiday left!

12 – All right – correct   Alright – wrong

Newspaper and televised advertisements, articles, letters and memoranda everywhere make use of *alright* and claim it to be a legitimate word. Some dictionaries approve it without reservation; others steer us down the middle with: *Alright* – Often the spelling of **all right.**

Make No Mistake accepts only **all right.** That is the stand taken by most editors. Even **all right** is colloquial – it is equivalent of the now universal American O.K. The foreign student would almost certainly understand O.K. sooner than a literal translation of **all right.**

Wrong	Corrected
If it's *alright* with you we will call at your office tomorrow to discuss the new contract.	If it's **all right** with you, we will call at your office tomorrow to discuss the new contract.
You appear to have lost a lot of weight in the last month. Are you *alright?*	You appear to have lost a lot of weight in the last month. Are you **all right?**
Everything is *alright* in the city today after last night's trouble.	Everything is **all right** in the city today after last night's trouble.

13 – Also

Also, meaning besides or as well as, is sometimes written to divide a sentence, as **and** is used to link two clauses. It is advisable that **and** should precede **also,** unless a semi-colon is placed in front of it to break the sentence *(see below).* ***Also*** is not a popular word with which to begin a sentence.

Wrong	Corrected
They bought a mahogany table ***also*** a new chair.	They bought a mahogany table **and also** a new chair.
Share prices have risen ***also*** the dollar has gained against most European currencies this week.	Share prices have risen; **also,** the dollar has gained against most European currencies this week.

14 – Alternative

Does **alternative** permit choice between **only two** things? Or can there be **several alternatives?** A hundred years ago there was only one alternative, but opinion and practice now overwhelm that old rule. We often read "Consider **those alternatives**". However, many writers still make the limit **one** alternative.

Unacceptable	Preferred
The ***other alternative*** to Trowbridge for the meeting is Chippenham.	The **alternative** to Trowbridge for the meeting is Chippenham.
Acceptable/disliked	**Preferred**
She will ring you to suggest ***alternative*** dates.	She will ring you to suggest **other possible** dates.
The council has at least ten ***alternatives*** to discuss when choosing a name for the new road.	When choosing a name for the new road, the council **will discuss at least ten suggestions.**
Our manager was given two ***alternatives*** – to resign or take a lesser post.	Our manager was told he could resign or take a lesser post.

15 – Alternate

Alternate, sometimes confused with alternative, means coming one after the other (every other) in turn: "Tom Burton visited Berlin in **alternate years** – 1989, 1991, 1993".

Wrong	Corrected
The *alternate date* of May 6 is rejected. May 3 and June 2 in *alternative years* will be used.	The **alternative date** of May 6 is rejected. May 3 and June 2 in **alternate years** will be used.
Half the women work here on *alternative days* – Mondays, Wednesdays and Fridays.	Half the women work here on **alternate days** – Mondays, Wednesdays and Fridays.

16 – Although or Though?

The meanings of **although** and **though** are similar. Many dictionaries simply render although as though, both defined as: in spite of the fact, notwithstanding. As conjunctions they are usually interchangeable, at the start of a sentence or clause. **Although** is preferred to begin a sentence.

Even is commonly placed in front of **though** for emphasis:

Tom will try to repair your cooker tonight, **even though** he may be tired after a hard day's work at the factory.

As though and **As if** are written to make a comparison:

The storm was frightening, **as though** (or **as if**) the world was about to end.

As an adverb, **though** (meaning however) often comes in the middle of a sentence or at the end:

Tim is honest – he has little ability as a salesman, **though.**

Reported	Preferred/Correct
Though I shall be away, rehearsals will continue.	**Although** I shall be away, rehearsals will continue.
The car crashed *even although* travelling slowly.	The car crashed **even though** travelling slowly.

17 – Altogether or All together?

Visitors to the United Kingdom are not the only people who find it difficult to understand the different meanings of these words. They are identical when spoken.

Altogether is understood to be without exception, totally, absolutely, utterly. "He has made a hash of that plan for his house **altogether.**"

All together puts the entire number of persons or things in one place and, possibly, at one time. "He has made a hash **altogether** of that plan for their new house, but I think the family will be able to put it right when they are **all together** next week."

Wrong	Corrected
The headmaster asked me to send the boys to see him in his study *altogether.*	The headmaster asked me to send the boys to see him in his study **all together.**
The carnival was *all together a fiasco.* The thunderstorm wrecked it.	The carnival was **altogether a fiasco.** The thunderstorm wrecked it.

18 – Amiable or Amicable?

Amiable is written usually to describe a person as friendly and likeable. **Amicable** is defined as a friendly, harmonious attitude to an arrangement between people, or the settlement of a dispute.

> A company rejected a claim for wrongful dismissal of an employee but **an amicable agreement** was reached without reference to lawyers or to an industrial tribunal.

Reported	Corrected
An amiable settlement about the fence will enable the two neighbours to live peacefully together.	**An amicable settlement** about the fence will enable the two neighbours to live peacefully together.
Jo Judd has such *an amicable disposition* that we shall welcome her into our choir.	Jo Judd has such **an amiable disposition** that we shall welcome her into our choir.

19 – Amount or Number?

The distinction should require little explanation but ***amount*** is often wrongly used for **number.** We hear that ***a large amount of members*** agreed or disagreed with something. Ugly.

Amount is associated with quantity in bulk, usually a substance without specific weight or size. "They bought **a large amount of flour** for the bakery." (A writer with a sense of detail would say how much. Four tonnes?)

Number is unlikely to be used wrongly for **amount** because it refers to single units. "They bought a **large number of bags** of flour for the bakery."

Wrong	Corrected
The amount of spectators at the World Cup was greater than expected.	**The number of spectators** at the World Cup was greater than expected.
If it is just ten pens you want, that is an ***amount*** I can find easily for you.	If it is just ten pens you want, that is a **number** I can find easily for you.

20 – Anybody / Anyone / Nobody / Someone / Somebody IS

Body and **one** are singular words. **Anybody, anyone, nobody, someone** and **somebody** should be followed by **is, was,** etc. That grammatical rule is broken in "Nobody knows that, ***do they?***" – an example of phrases accepted here only as a colloquialism.

Wrong	Corrected
Nobody among thousands here ***are*** likely to win anything.	**Nobody** among thousands here **is** likely to win anything.
Could ***anybody*** ever think of betraying ***their*** country?	Could **anybody** ever think of betraying **his or her** country?
Anyone from the Women's Institute can put ***their*** name down for the course.	**Anyone** from the Women's Institute can put **her** name down for the course.
Somebody sent £1000 in cash anonymously. We shall never know who ***they were.***	**Somebody** sent £1000 in cash anonymously. We shall never know who **it was.**

21 – Anyone or Any One?

At first sight they look the same, and errors are, perhaps, understandable. But there is a difference – a difference which also applies to **anything/any thing** and **everyone/every one** etc.

Any one are written as two words when the emphasis is on one, as would be the case with **any two, any three, any seven** and so on. Example:

They could buy **any one** of the nine cars on offer.

Anyone refers to persons, not things, and is not normally followed by ***of.*** It is singular but can refer to a whole population. "The door is open and **anyone** is welcome."

Wrong	Corrected
Any one over 18 is eligible to join the new social club in our village.	**Anyone over 18** is eligible to join the new social club in our village.
Anyone of the company's *six salesmen* has the ability to become the sales' manager.	**Any one** of the company's **six salesmen** has the ability to become the sales' manager.

22 – Arise or Rise?

They are interchangeable nine times out of ten. But there is a difference. A difficulty over a boy's education **arises** when he plays truant from school.

We shall **arise** at dawn to go fishing; that is not misuse of the verb but is old-fashioned. We **rise** (get up) is much better. Wages and temperatures **rise** (they go up). Wages and temperatures **arise** as subjects for discussion.

Reported	Corrected
The sun arises over the North Sea to the east of Lowestoft.	**The sun rises** over the North Sea to the east of Lowestoft.
Opportunities for better jobs *rise* when a young man obtains qualifications, whether in a craft or in a profession.	**Opportunities** for better jobs **arise** when a young man obtains qualifications, whether in a craft or in a profession.

23 – Around or Round?

Both **around** and **round** have meanings connected with circles or movement; but only **around** is used for approximately. "It happened **around midnight.**"

The basic definition of **round** is circular or spherical in shape, but it is written frequently with metaphorical meanings. We refer to **a round** trip, **rounding up** sheep, **a round** of drinks, **a round** of golf, the **first round** of a competition, **turning round** to see something, **a round** in the boxing ring.

Around = on every side, about; often interchangeable with **round.** Preferred to round in the USA. "They **came around** to see me yesterday. John knows **his way around** Cape Town."

Reported	Preferred
Josephine turned around and saw a man drive off in her car. She had seen him *round.* The boxer was knocked unconscious but came *around in two or three minutes.*	**Josephine turned round** and saw a man drive off in her car. She had seen him **around.** The boxer was knocked unconscious but came **round in two or three minutes.**

24 – Artist or Artiste?

An artist is usually a painter of pictures *(Goya)* or sculptor *(Henry Moore).* A talented craftsman may be described as an artist; for instance, a potter who makes earthenware vessels with taste and skill. Many writers, especially newspaper journalists, have given the word a broader meaning, applying it to footballers, authors and others.

An artiste is an entertainer – a singer *(Pavarotti),* an actress *(Elizabeth Taylor),* a dancer *(Nureyev). Artiste* is not the feminine of **artist,** as is sometimes assumed.

Wrong	Corrected
The artists at the Theatre Royal this week include ballet dancers as well as opera singers. The theatre's *artistes* have created superb scenes with brush and paint.	**The artistes** at the Theatre Royal this week include ballet dancers as well as opera singers. The theatre's **artists** have created superb scenes with brush and paint.

25 – The Aspirate (when h is not sounded)

In pronunciation, the aspirate is the sound of the letter **h** created by heavier breathing. It is usually the first letter of a word but there can be an effective **h** within it. If at the beginning, **a**, not *an*, is in front.

a harp   a hasty word   a helpful man   a local inhabitant

There are exceptions. The **h** is silent in hour, heir, honour, honest and in words from the same source (hourly, heiress, heirloom, honourable, honorary, honestly, honesty). Herb and humble once had the silent **h** and some people still write and say "an historic year, an hotel, an horrendous moment".

Wrong	Corrected
Sam, ***a honest man,*** rejected ***a honorary position*** as the club's secretary, because he saw dishonesty in the huge expenses offered as enticement to take the job.	Sam, **an honest man,** rejected **an honorary position** as the club's secretary, because he saw dishonesty in the huge expenses offered as enticement to take the job.

26 – Assault or Insult?

An insult is a spoken or gesticulated attack. The people insulted are treated with gross indignity, abused with insolence, scorn and contempt, with such statements as: "You haven't the intelligence of a pig or the courage of a rabbit".

An assault is a physical attack, which may be with the hands, an instrument or even a gun, on one person or more. It may also be the action of an army upon an army in time of war or crowd upon crowd, as has happened at football matches.

Wrong	Corrected
It was a blatant ***assault*** to accuse George, my partner, of cheating in the game of cards at my club. The Rugby match became a riot, with fists and boots flying – the worst ***insults*** ever seen at Prebble Park.	It was a blatant **insult** to accuse George, my partner, of cheating in the game of cards at my club. The Rugby match became a riot, with fists and boots flying – the worst **assaults** ever seen at Prebble Park.

27 – At or In or On?

A writer's choice is wide here, and the three words are discussed only in their application as prepositions in terms of time, place and space.

Do we write "**in** Birmingham, **at** North Petherwin, **on** the Equator"? The answer is "Yes", but the use of all three can be interpreted broadly. "We stayed one night **at** Felixstowe" will read and sound as correct as "We stayed one night **in** Felixstowe".

Advice over the years, particularly from the editors of newspapers, which use them most, has been:

1 – Write **at** when referring to a point on the map such as a village or small town. "The coach stopped **at** the villages of Werrington and Whitstone on the way to Bude."

2 – Write **in** when the place named gives the reader an impression of space, such as a large town, city, province or country. "You will need good maps if you plan to drive **in** Manchester or **in** Sydney."

3 – Write **on** as **upon** might be used: **On** the manager's desk. He is not dependent **on** anyone.

4 – Stating time is a little complicated. We write:

AT 5pm	IN the morning	ON Saturday
four o'clock	the spring	November 5th
Christmas	December	my birthday
the week-end	1995	Christmas Day
night		

Statement	**Preferred**
At London we were looking at Nelson's Column *on* Trafalgar Square when three police cars passed along the Embankment at high speed. They had been called to quell trouble among a large crowd attending a protest meeting *at* Clapham Common.	**In** London we were looking at Nelson's Column **in** Trafalgar Square when three police cars passed along the Embankment at high speed. They had been called to quell trouble among a large crowd attending a protest meeting **on** Clapham Common.
The plane landed *in* Stansted airport and we spent the night *at* London.	The plane landed **at** Stansted airport and we spent the night **in** London.

28 – Autobiography or Biography?

The life-story of a person written by himself or herself – an **autobiography** is sometimes described wrongly as a **biography,** which is a similar personal history but written by another, with or without co-operation or consent.

In modern times, professional writers "ghost" probably half the autobiographies. They act for the autobiographer from information provided. That is especially true of sporting personalities, who usually seek a highly-controversial angle that will appeal to reviewers of books and attract newspaper serial rights.

The first biographer who comes to mind is James Boswell (1740-95). His classic (1791) about Samuel Johnson, poet, critic and compiler of *A Dictionary of the English Language* (1755), created the adjective Boswellian, which appears in dictionaries; it appraises someone.

Wrong	Corrected
H. Montgomery-Hyde wrote an excellent ***autobiography*** about Norman Birkett, a barrister and judge of distinction in the mid-20th century.	H. Montgomery-Hyde wrote an excellent **biography** about Norman Birkett, a barrister and judge of distinction in the mid-20th century.

29 – Averse or Adverse?

These adjectives are close. Both have acquired two or three similar synonyms, declaring opposition. **Averse** = opposed, reluctant, disinclined, loth. "Some politicians have become **averse** to the idea of a federal Europe."

Adverse is unfavourable, hostile, critical. A student's work may bring **adverse comment** in an end-of-term appraisal.

Wrong	Corrected
The factory workers are so ***adverse*** to taking their holidays in two parts that they have sent an ***averse*** report about their company to their local MP.	The factory workers are so **averse** to taking their holidays in two parts that they have sent an **adverse** report about their company to their local MP.

30 – Award or Reward?

The meanings are near enough to confuse. An applicant in a court case might be **awarded** £500 as recompense for damage to his car. He was not ***rewarded,*** unless we interpret the money as reward for the physical and mental effort required to apply.

An award and **to award** are used not only in legal matters. A prize can be **awarded** for the best horse in the show.

A reward and **to reward** express recognition of some commendable act or achievement, with money or token. **Rewards** are usually associated with the return of lost property to its owner or for information leading to the arrest of criminals.

Wrong	Corrected
The judge fined Jack £800 and ***rewarded*** the victim ***with*** £300 compensation.	The judge fined Jack £800 and **awarded** the victim £300 compensation.
The insurance company paid ***an award*** to the man whose clues led to the recovery of the stolen gold.	The insurance company paid **a reward** to the man whose clues led to the recovery of the stolen gold.
His father was ***rewarded*** the Military Medal in World War I.	His father was **awarded** the Military Medal in World War I.
Naomi trained every day for the 400 metres' race and was ***awarded*** today with victory.	Naomi trained every day for the 400 metres' race and was **rewarded** today with victory.

31 – Bare or Bear?

Written as an adjective: "The pantry is **bare** (empty)". "She was bare (naked) in the bathroom when a robber struck." As a verb: "They **bared** (uncovered) their heads in memory of the dead".

To bear is to suffer, to endure, to yield, to carry, to give birth to.

Wrong	Corrected
I cannot ***bare*** the thought of your bad luck.	I cannot **bear** the thought of your bad luck.

32 – Beach or Beech?

Errors are many. **Beach** is the sandy or pebbly seashore from which we bathe or on which we sit. **Beech** is a tree with a smooth bark, with leaves that are a lovely autumnal sight.

Wrong	Corrected
The wreck left the ***beech*** strewn with wood, some of it branches of ***beach*** trees.	The wreck left the **beach** strewn with wood, some of it branches of **beech** trees.

33 – Between or Among?

The old general rule is to write: (1) **Between two** and (2) **among three** (or more). But time has eaten away old-time grammar and **between** now often deals with more than two of anything. It is used for individual relationships (**between** father, mother and son).

The argument that *among* is sometimes not appropriate and should give way to **between** has to be accepted, as in:

> The winners will be decided **between** the choirs from France, Hungary, Italy, Austria, Chile, South Africa and Brazil.

Note that we write "Between one thing **and** another" and not "Between one thing *or* another."

Reported	Correct
The millionaire's Will divided the fortune equally ***between four sons.***	The millionaire's Will divided the fortune equally **among four sons.**
The Will divided the fortune equally ***among two sons.***	The Will divided the fortune equally **between two sons.**
I had to decide ***between*** redundancies ***or*** ending all overtime.	I had to decide **between** redundancies **and** ending all overtime.
They chose ***between five*** men when electing Horace.	They chose **from among five** men when electing Horace.
Between each hilltop the fires burned.	**Between the hilltops** the fires burned.

34 – Between you and me – right Between you and I – wrong

Between you and I is often spoken, wrongly – sometimes through ignorance, sometimes by a pretentious person who thinks **"I"** gives an impression of superiority. **Between you and me** is correct, as is **Between him and her.**

Grammatical error is heard clearly enough if we say ***"Between I and you"*** or ***"Between she and they".***

Wrong	Corrected
Father made a new Will and all his assets will now be divided ***between we and they.***	Father made a new Will and all his assets will now be divided **between us and them.**
Between you and I, we have been told that our neighbours are not married.	**Between you and me,** we have been told that our neighbours are not married.

35 – Biennial or Biannual or Perennial?

All three words are commonly associated with botany but are also widely used in other areas. Two flow from the prefix **bi-**, which means twice, doubly, two.

Biennial denotes that something happens once in two years. An inspection of a police force may take place every two years, **biennially. A biennial** plant produces roots and leaves the first year, flowers and fruit the second year, then dies.

Biannual tells us that something happens twice a year. Many associations have **biannual** meetings or outings.

A **perennial** plant continues through many years, always expected to last much longer than two years. The meaning is perpetual, never ceasing.

Wrong	Corrected
Our Chamber of Commerce's ***annual*** visit to Scarborough will become ***biannual*** after this year. We have to save money, so there will be no treat for members and their wives next year.	Our Chamber of Commerce's **annual** visit to Scarborough will become **biennial** after this year. We have to save money, so there will be no treat for members and their wives next year.

36 – Bilateral or Unilateral?

The definition of **lateral** is "of, pertaining to, proceeding from, directed towards the side". As **bi-** denotes two and **uni-** is one, the meanings unfold.

Bilateral is two-sided. **A bilateral agreement** binds the two parties to fulfil all obligations contained therein.

Unilateral affects only one side or party. Ian Smith, then Prime Minister of Rhodesia, made **a unilateral declaration** of independence, to be known worldwide as UDI.

Wrong	Corrected
The *unilateral contract* will benefit *both* companies; it assures equal profits.	The **bilateral** contract will benefit both companies; it assures equal profits.

37 – A Billion?

Billion: A million millions. That definition is from 30 dictionaries published between 1921 and 1990. In figures: 1,000,000 × 1,000,000 = 1,000,000,000,000, (abbreviation, 1bn).

But 1bn is now officially defined in the United Kingdom as a thousand millions, i.e. 1,000 × 1,000,000 = 1,000,000,000.

Hints of the change began to appear in the 1980s. Some dictionaries, having defined billion as a **million millions,** followed with: **thousand millions** (United States' usage, increasingly British). The latest dictionaries print: thousand millions (formerly million millions).

Any writer presenting a country's trade deficit or surplus (£10.9bn), or a company's turnover or profit (£1.1bn), or a foreign currency total (DM36bn) must beware of possible misunderstandings. Dictionaries, in tens of thousands, are still in use with the original interpretation. Particularly vulnerable to errors and consequent statistical misjudgments are students whose English is a second language.

The old	The new
Receipts last year were £22,000,000,000 (£0.022bn).	Receipts last year were £22,000,000,000 (£22bn).

38 – Bore or Boor?

A bore *(noun)* is a dull person who wearies others with tedious talk. He or she may be an acqaintance, a politician, a preacher, a teacher or a salesman. Some of them **bore** *(verb)* **us** on radio and television.

A boor can be an uneducated, coarse person, whom we describe as **boorish** *(adjective).*

Wrong	Corrected
You *boor* me to tears with that talk about those rounds of golf.	You **bore** me to tears with that talk about those rounds of golf.

39 – Born or Borne

Both **born** and **borne** are past participles of the verb **bear** *(see bare/bear, page 67).* Some grammarians regard **bear,** when used to mean "give birth" as old fashioned – "She **bore** him two sons" – but it is still seen and heard. The more common use is in the passive – "Churchill **was born** in 1874". Someone can also be described as a **born musician** or a **born hypocrite.**

Borne is sometimes incorrectly written as **born** when the meaning intended is to carry. Correct usage: (a) "Ada asked me **to bear the trunk** into the house for her"; (b) "He **bore the trunk** indoors for her"; (c) "The injured man was **borne** into the hospital **on a stretcher**". An illness may be **borne** with courage.

Wrong	Corrected
As I had *born the cost* of the Christmas party five times already, it was my brother's turn to bear some of it this year. *The child was borne* at 0700 hours and was immediately *born across the road* to the intensive care unit.	As I had **borne the cost** of the Christmas party five times already, it was my brother's turn to bear some of it this year. **The child was born** at 0700 hours and was immediately **borne across the road** to the intensive care unit.

Bourne, meaning limit, has almost the same pronunciation as born and borne. Only misspelling creates confusion.

40 – Break or Brake?

They are distant relatives. **To break** is to shatter, to destroy. A glass breaks if dropped. **To brake** is to apply a device to check the speed of a wheel or vehicle, possibly to stop it, using the **brakes** *(noun).*

Wrong	Corrected
The breaks failed and the car went on to ***brake*** through a garden fence.	**The brakes failed** and the car went on to **break** through a garden fence.
He broke too hard and his cycle skidded out of control in the mud.	**He braked too hard** and his cycle skidded out of control in the mud.
She braked too many ***glasses*** while serving beer in the bar of our hotel.	**She broke** too many **glasses** while serving beer in the bar of our hotel.

41 – But

The two familiar uses for **but** are: (1) As a conjunction linking two parts of a sentence that are a contrast ("He is **strict but fair**") and (2) as a preposition meaning except ("Everyone has given money to the famine fund **but him**"). A grammatical point in (2) is that him, **him/her** etc., not ***he/she*** etc., normally follow a preposition, although **he/she** etc. follow in a sentence such as "The lights went out when all **but he** had spoken".

Words such as ***however*** and ***nevertheless*** should not be used in the same sentence as **but;** they convey a similar meaning.

Wrong	Corrected
The family all voted for Owen Jones ***but I.***	The family all voted for Owen Jones **but me.**
They felt very cold driving through the mountains ***and*** arrived home safely.	They felt very cold driving through the mountains **but** arrived home safely.
He tried to rescue the swimmer ***but failed, however,*** to reach her.	He tried to rescue the swimmer **but failed** to reach her.

Learning by Example

COMMON MISTAKES

Part two – C to D

42 – Calendar or Calender?

Confusion leads to misspellings but little misunderstanding because **calender** is an uncommon word, being a press with rollers used in the manufacture of cloth – a steam mangle.

A calendar is an almanac, a table of days and months of the year. A month is 28 days/four weeks. A year, January to December is 12 **calendar** months. **Calendar** is also a list of cases to be heard in a criminal court. **To calendar** is to enter in a list.

Wrong	Corrected
The calendar broke down and it will be two *calender months* before work resumes. Five judges now sitting at the Crown Court face thc heaviest *calender* yet, including four murders.	**The calender broke down** and it will be two **calendar months** before work resumes. Five judges now sitting at the Crown Court face the heaviest **calendar** yet, including four murders.

43 – Can or May?

In speech, pitch of the voice will convey **can** to mean **may,** regardless of definitions, but there are differences. **Can** expresses ability/capability, having the skill or knowledge to do something. "I know you **can** repair that window frame." **Can** also means to do or to see something because permission has been given. "I **can** visit the botanical gardens even when they are not open to the public."

May expresses possibility, likelihood, to have the physical or moral opportunity to do something. "You **may** already possess the secret formula for our new product, for all I know." It is similar to **can** when used in the sense of to be free to, to be permitted to. "You **may** have a banana if you are hungry."

Reported	Intended meaning/Preferred
You can find that trains to Gunton no longer run on Sunday mornings.	**You may find** that trains to Gunton no longer run on Sunday mornings.
May you identify those wild flowers and mushrooms we found in Epping Forest?	**Can you identify** those wild flowers and mushrooms we found in Epping Forest?

44 – Canon or Cannon?

Canon law is church law. **Canon Edward Hope** is a senior clergyman. **Canon** can also mean a rule, standard or principle.

A cannon is a big gun; also a scoring stroke in the game of billiards, when the cue ball strikes the other two. **To cannon,** meaning to collide or to ricochet, is commonly used.

Wrong	Corrected
Canon to right of them, *Canon* to left of them, *Canon* in front of them. Volley'd and thunder'd.	**Cannon** to right of them, **Cannon** to left of them, **Cannon** in front of them. Volley'd and thunder'd. – *Tennyson*
Tom scored 27 consecutive *canons* in his game of billiards with *Cannon* Low, and won easily.	Tom scored 27 consecutive **cannons** in his game of billiards with **Canon** Low, and won easily.

45 – Canvas or Canvass?

Unless a dictionary is handy, some of us have had to guess which to write. Without checking, mistakes are possible.

Canvas *(noun)* is a closely-woven fabric used as floor covering, as sails and as a surface for oil-painting.

To canvass *(verb)* is a word constantly spoken and written at election time. It means to solicit votes, opinions or orders for merchandise. A salesman **canvasses for orders.**

Wrong	Corrected
Will you *canvas* support to impose a speed limit here?	Will you **canvass** support to impose a speed limit here?
We used to sell *canvass* for all floors, but carpets are the fashion these days.	We used to sell **canvas** for all floors, but carpets are the fashion these days.

46 – Capital letters

No rule dictates all uses of capital letters, but one should start every sentence and be written uniformly in any text.

Names of organisations and titles take capital letters – the National Union of Journalists, the Prime Minister, Professor Eric Jenkins, the Green Party, Afforn Town Council. Lower case letters are preferred when there is no name or title. Examples:

> Ardop Football Club appointed a new manager, who has not yet been named. The **club** will call a press conference.
>
> Professor Eric Jenkins will retire at the end of the university's academic year. There will be no replacement for two years. The **professor** intends to remain in the area.

Religious references require capital letters: God, the Almighty, the Bible, the Gospels, the Scriptures, the Koran.

Reported	Preferred
Afforn District Council meets today to discuss the new rate. ....The *Council* may impose a 10 per cent increase.	Afforn District Council meets today to discuss the new rate. ....The **council** may impose a 10 per cent increase.

47 – Catholic with a small c or capital C?

Care is needed in use of **catholic** with a small c (meaning liberal, universal, comprehensive) and **Catholic** with a capital C (used in the religious context, embracing all Christian Churches).

A person may have a **catholic sympathy** for all religions and may not be **a Roman Catholic.**

Wrong	Corrected
Tom, who is a Roman *catholic* and has met the Pope, has *Catholic* tastes for food – and a good appetite. Roast beef and Yorkshire pudding will please him best, but fish or poultry will satisfy him.	Tom, who is a Roman **Catholic** and has met the Pope, has **catholic** tastes for food – and a good appetite. Roast beef and Yorkshire pudding will please him best, but fish or poultry will satisfy him.

48 – Choose or Chose or Chosen?

Errors in the meaning of **to choose** (i.e., to select something where there is an option, to prefer, to decide to follow a particular career or action) are rare. Errors in choosing the right tense are common. We should write: **"I choose my friends** wisely. As a child **I chose my friends** wisely. **I have chosen my friends** wisely".

The noun, **choice,** is the product of what has been chosen, but it has another meaning as an adjective – excellent, superior. "She was presented with **a choice basket of fruit**."

Wrong	Corrected
I always *chose* new shoes carefully since I *choose* an expensive pair two years ago and they became too big when the leather softened. They have *chose* the wrong colour for the front door of their new house. I do not admire their choice.	I always **choose** new shoes carefully since I **chose** an expensive pair two years ago and they became too big when the leather softened. They have **chosen** the wrong colour for the front door of their new house. I do not admire their choice.

49 – Civil or Civic?

A civil person is courteous and non-military. This adjective is also found in **Civil Service** (the country's administrators), **civil disobedience** (e.g., members of a community refusing to pay a tax), **civil war** (citizens of the same state at war), **civil engineer** (one who constructs roads etc.).

Civic relates to a city or citizenship. A city hall is the **civic headquarters.**

Wrong	Corrected
Most countries have a *civic* airline, some with airfields owned by the *civil* authority.	Most countries have a **civil** airline, some with airfields owned by the **civic** authority.

50 – Climatic or Climactic?

Climatic is the adjective of climate, which is the weather in any area. **Climatic conditions** can spoil open-air enjoyment.

Climactic is the adjective of climax, which can be the chapter in a story where crisis is reached or solved, the turning point of a career or fulfilment of an ambition.

Wrong	Corrected
The storm's *climatic* moment was that huge thunderbolt.	The storm's **climactic** moment was that huge thunderbolt.

51 – Coarse or Course?

Coarse *(adjective)*: gross, unrefined, vulgar (behaviour), rough (cloth). **Course** *(noun)*: part of a meal, the direction taken, a series of lessons or areas where golf is played or races run. **To course,** the verb, is to hunt with hounds.

Wrong	Corrected
Our guest is in the *coarse* of eating ten cakes. You see how *course* he is.	Our guest is in the **course** of eating ten cakes. You see how **coarse** he is.

52 – The Committee/Council/Team was or were?

Styles for COLLECTIVE NOUNS in publishing houses, newspaper offices and grammarians' heads vary but there are rules accepted generally:

1 – If the collection of persons or objects is seen as one mass, **is** or **was** is preferred.

The public **is** not admitted.

The nation **is** alert to a threat to its security.

2 – When reference is to one unit but individual action is obvious, **were** or **are** is more appropriate.

The council *(the councillors)* **are** now debating the financial crisis.

The team *(the players)* **were** in great form last night.

People in those examples are shown in (1) as singular and in (2) as plural. The difference, however, is thin between the two interpretations. It would not be wrong to write:

The council **has** referred the matter to the Minister.

The council **was** divided on the appointment and **has** postponed a decision until next week.

The trend is towards use of the plural, especially in sport. Some years ago, *The Times*, of London, then regarded as judge and jury of the English language, always wrote **"The team was"**. Now its style is **"The team were"**.

Reported	Preferred
The committee of inquiry *were* headed by a High Court judge.	**The committee** of inquiry **was** headed by a High Court judge.
Our battalion were sent into battle with too few tanks, but victory came quickly.	**Our battalion was** sent into battle with too few tanks, but victory came quickly.
The public at today's rally *is* expected to behave better than last year's rowdy crowd.	**The public** at today's rally **are** expected to behave better than last year's rowdy crowd.
The match is off because *the team does* not want to play during the Easter holiday.	The match is off because **the team do** not want to play during the Easter holiday.

53 – Compare to or Compare with?

Compare to = liken to, look at the similarities. The degree of equality, likeness or similarity is suggested. There is a comparison. Example:

She is a contralto and I **compare** her voice **to** the voice of the late Kathleen Ferrier.

Compare with points to and examines two persons or objects, seeking either likeness or difference. Is there a comparison? Example:

He **compared** me **with** Pele and everybody laughed at his description of the different way I play football.

Likeness to Pele is not suggested, merely that a comparison is being made, with the laughter at my expense!

Meaning not intended	Intended meaning
We compare our research ***to*** that of our French partners before publishing a report.	**We compare** our research **with** that of our French partners before publishing a report.
I ***compare*** your hairstyle ***with*** my haystack!	I **compare** your hairstyle **to** my haystack!

54 – Compliment or Complement?

The gap in meaning is broad. Many mistakes are seen in print and in letters. **Compliment** *(noun and verb)* means praise.

The President paid us a **compliment** *(noun)* by sending a gift and **complimented** *(verb)* the organisers on their efforts.

Complement, as a verb, completes a number **(to complement).** Used as a noun, the number is completed **(the complement).**

I hear you have a full **complement** *(noun)* of guests coming for the wedding. My car will **complement** *(verb)* your transport.

Wrong	Corrected
Complement Joan on passing her music examination.	**Compliment Joan** on passing her music examination.
The full compliment needed to start the race is 20 men.	**The full complement** needed to start the race is 20 men.

55 – Compose or Comprise?

The difference is narrow. **To compose** is to make up, to put together elements or parts, to originate in music or literature. "The jig-saw puzzle is **composed of** 164 pieces."

To comprise is to consist of, to contain, to include. Note the difference: "The jig-saw puzzle **comprises** 164 pieces".

Wrong	Corrected
Our plant research unit at the university ***composes*** a pathologist, a virologist and a microbiologist.	Our plant research unit at the university **comprises** a pathologist, a virologist and a microbiologist.
The family we met in York was ***comprised of*** eight children, two parents and a grandmother.	The family we met in York was **composed of** eight children, two parents and a grandmother.

56 – Conservative with a small c or capital C?

To write of **conservative policies** is not necessarily reference to a **Conservative Party** manifesto. **Conservative** with a small c is entirely non-party political – an adjective or noun in common use, meaning commitment to uphold the existing order of things, dislike of violent or radical change.

Beware of one minor danger. Sentences begin with a capital letter and this one, written thoughtlessly, might create misunderstanding:

> **Conservative thinking** in the village about the route of the new by-pass to be built next year is that it will inflict permanent damage on Northamptonshire countryside of great natural beauty. Many young people reject that view.

Are those thinkers in the village **Conservative Party** members or non-political **conservationists**? We do not know.

Meaning not intended	Meaning intended
The casting vote of one old ***Conservative***-minded member caused our council to reject plans for a new town hall.	The casting vote of one old **conservative**-minded member caused our council to reject plans for a new town hall.

57 – Conserve or Preserve?

They are synonyms to the extent of being interchangeable in most cases. **Conservation societies** in the United Kingdom and other countries have the same functions as **preservation societies.**

Conserve: To reserve, to save (physical energy, fuel), to retain (woodland), to hoard (food supply for an emergency).

Preserve: To protect from decline in quality or quantity (fruit, buildings, pictures), to prevent alteration to an antique article or to an old property. In some countries authorities place **preservation orders** on buildings and trees.

Unacceptable	Correct
I shall not train today but rest at home ***to preserve*** my strength for tomorrow's London marathon.	I shall not train today but rest at home **to conserve** my strength for tomorrow's London marathon.
To conserve those lovely Chippendale chairs from further decay we need to consult an expert.	**To preserve** those lovely Chippendale chairs from further decay we need to consult an expert.

58 – Consist of or Consist in?

The prepositions **of** and **in** give **consist** different meanings. **To consist of** is to be made up of, to comprise. "My house **consists of** seven rooms, a garage and a large garden."

To consist in is to be part of, to have as its foundation, substance or nature. "My problem **consists in** living too far from my work and having to leave home too early."

Wrong	Corrected
Our football club ***consists in*** only eleven experienced players and one coach.	Our football club **consists of** only eleven experienced players and one coach.
The pleasure of living on the island ***consists of*** a simple life.	The pleasure of living on the island **consists in** a simple life.

59 – Continuous or Continual?

The difference is thin but important if an exact meaning is needed. **Continuous** is happening all the time, without a break, uninterrupted.

A campaign against race discrimination, known as apartheid in South Africa, was **continuous** for most of the 20th century.

Continual: Almost without break, often repeated. A football match may be **continuous** but spectators' cheers only **continual.**

The rains were **continual** last summer, leaving us with few days when we could play tennis without interruption.

Wrong	Corrected
We started the engine at 8am and it had ***a continual run*** until 8pm the next day.	We started the engine at 8am and it had **a continuous run** until 8pm the next day.
The baby's ***continuous crying*** every hour or so through the night spoilt our holiday.	The baby's **continual crying** every hour or so through the night spoilt our holiday.

60 – Correspond with or Correspond to?

To correspond with Margaret Smith is to exchange letters with her. A South African statesman's attitude to racism now **corresponds to** (i.e., is similar to) his abhorrence of township violence in some parts of his country.

With can often be written instead of **to.** "My salary does not **correspond with/to** yours." But **to** is preferred to ***with*** where choice can be made.

Reported	Preferred
We have ***corresponded to*** a Hungarian family for years, and we shall see them soon as they are coming here.	We have **corresponded with** a Hungarian family for years, and we shall see them soon as they are coming here.
Receipts at today's show do not ***correspond with*** last year's record. We are at least £500 short.	Receipts at today's show do not **correspond to** (tally with) last year's record. We are at least £500 short.

61 – Correspondent or Co-respondent?

A correspondent is a writer of letters. **A co-respondent** is the third party in a divorce action cited as having committed adultery with the husband or wife.

Wrong	Corrected
I was the ***co-respondent*** who wrote the report for the *Daily Gazette,* making those allegations of adultery. The ***correspondent*** did not deny them at the court hearing.	I was the **correspondent** who wrote the report for the *Daily Gazette* about those allegations of adultery. The **co-respondent** did not deny them at the court hearing.

62 – Council or Counsel?

Mistakes occur when **council** or **counsel** is dictated to a secretary without clarifying **-cil** or **-sel.**

Council is an assembly of councillors who administer the affairs of a parish, town, county or any organisation. Essex County Council, Broadland District Council, the Sports Council and the Arts Council are among hundreds.

Counsel is advice, and also the name given to a barrister-at-law (e.g., a QC is a Queen's Counsel). **To counsel** is to give advice – given by a counsellor.

Wrong	Corrected
The priest was immediately at the side of the bereaved ***to give council,*** and he has promised to organise a petition to the ***counsel,*** pleading for improvements to the road where the accident happened and four children were killed. ***The counsel's waste disposal services*** broke down because the committee did not heed the ***council*** of its most experienced officer.	The priest was immediately at the side of the bereaved **to give counsel,** and he has promised to organise a petition to the **council,** pleading for improvements to the road where the accident happened and four children were killed. **The council's waste disposal services** broke down because the committee did not heed the **counsel** of its most experienced officer.

63 – Credible or Creditable?

A newspaper report is **credible** (to be believed) if it is true. The editor's decision to publish a report in defiance of pressure from influential outside sources that provide advertising revenue is **creditable** (merits praise, honourable).

The opposites to credible and creditable are **incredible** and **discreditable.**

Wrong meaning	Correct
The judge said the evidence of only one of the witnesses was *creditable,* and the jury acquitted both men.	The judge said the evidence of only one of the witnesses was **credible,** and the jury acquitted both men.
The most credible act during a disturbance at the prison was the courage of the priest, who went among the rioters and negotiated their surrender.	**The most creditable act** during a disturbance at the prison was the courage of the priest, who went among the rioters and negotiated their surrender.
An incredible business deal was agreed when one of the firms knew that it was already bankrupt.	**A discreditable business deal** was agreed when one of the firms knew that it was already bankrupt.

64 – Customer or Client?

A client is a customer and a customer is a client. But there is a shade of difference that determines their usage. **A customer** is usually someone who buys something from a shop or factory. **A client** is usually one who uses the services of a professional person (a lawyer, an accountant).

A surveyor's **clients** are known as his **clientele,** a noun that is also sometimes written to refer to a shopkeeper's customers.

Reported	Preferred
The grocer, who has at least five hundred *clients,* is to enlarge his premises and has become a *customer* of our architectural practice.	The grocer, who has at least five hundred **customers,** is to enlarge his premises and has become a **client** of our architectural practice.

65 – Debrief or Interrogate?

To brief is to provide information, to instruct. **To debrief** is to obtain information. It is a word now used widely, but was seen in few dictionaries until late this century.

A lawyer is **briefed** when the facts of a dispute or incident are passed to him or her. Criminal or civil court proceedings are then usually imminent against someone.

A person will be **debriefed** on returning from a mission (e.g., flight into space) or incarceration (e.g., held hostage in a foreign country). Questioning is likely to be friendly.

To interrogate is to question, often to try to obtain facts that are not likely to be volunteered. The interrogation, unlike debriefing, may be insistent, even hostile.

Wrong	Corrected
Detective-sergeant Smithdale decided ***to debrief*** seven youths suspected of setting fire to a haystack.	Detective-sergeant Smithdale decided **to interrogate** seven youths suspected of setting fire to a haystack.

66 – Definite or Definitive?

The date on which John Bone will take up a job with the council **is now definite** – June 1st. That is certain, exact, clear.

University researchers have published a paper identifying a virus in mushrooms. **Their findings are definitive** – i.e., conclusive, positive, final, unconditional.

Wrong	Corrected
Is Jim coming to my birthday party on Saturday? I would like ***a definitive answer*** now.	Is Jim coming to my birthday party on Saturday? I would like **a definite answer** now.
The House of Lords, as the Supreme Court of Appeal, makes judgments that are ***definite.*** The principles of those decisions are binding on lower courts. They are known as Case law.	The House of Lords, as the Supreme Court of Appeal, makes judgments that are **definitive.** The principles of those decisions are binding on lower courts. They are known as Case law.

67 – Delusion or Illusion?

A person can suffer either **a delusion** or **an illusion** that he or she is better qualified than other candidates to be the local Member of Parliament. The words are often interchangeable but meanings are a little different.

Delusion is a mistaken belief. In some cases it is fiction, a hallucination, even ridden with malice.

Illusion is less dramatic – a much milder self-deception, such as that created by a magician when he purports to saw a woman in half.

Reported	Preferred
You suffer ***an illusion*** in claiming to all around you that you have won the cup, before your horse has been judged. Your idea that small shops are better off now than they were 50 years ago is ***a delusion.***	You suffer **a delusion** in claiming to all around you that you have won the cup, before your horse has been judged. Your idea that small shops are better off now than they were 50 years ago is **an illusion.**

68 – Dependant or Dependent?

Dependant *(noun)* is someone, perhaps a 10-year-old girl, reliant on another or others. A childless couple may have adopted her. She is **dependent** *(the adjective)* on them for maintenance and is controlled by them.

Wrong	Corrected
The success of the horse show is ***dependant on the weather*** more than on the number of competitors. Florrie is now ***a dependent*** of Mr and Mrs Robinson, who have adopted her after long legal negotiations.	The success of the horse show is **dependent on the weather** more than on the number of competitors. Florrie is now a **dependant** of Mr and Mrs Robinson, who have adopted her after long legal negotiations.

69 – Desert or Dessert?

Desert and **dessert** cause as much confusion as any pair of words. They are in the canvas/canvass category for doubt.

Desert *(noun)* is a wilderness, such as the **Sahara Desert.** The verb **desert** abandons a place, position, people or person **(desert the Army, desert one's wife). Deserts** can mean a reward or a deserved punishment. "He had his **deserts** coming to him."

Dessert presents no problems. It is simply the fruit or sweetmeats that follow a meal.

Wrong	Corrected
We had lunch under a blazing sun in the *dessert* and even had coffee after the *desert.*	We had lunch under a blazing sun in the **desert** and even had coffee after the **dessert.**
He is an Army *desserter.* He has been absent from his regiment for six months.	He is an Army **deserter.** He has been absent from his regiment for six months.
If father *desserts* mother, I shall not speak to him again.	If father **deserts** mother, I shall not speak to him again.

70 – Detract or Distract?

To detract is to lessen in value. A person's character or appearance is disparaged, defamed, belittled, possibly slandered. The noun: **detraction** (disparagement, depreciation).

To distract a person is to take his or her attention away from an act, exercise or conversation. It is the creation of a diversion. The noun, **distraction,** is in common use with a meaning that ranges from bewilderment and anger to diversion.

Wrong	Corrected
He did not get the job, mainly because his dirty clothes *distracted* from his appearance when interviewed.	He did not get the job, mainly because his dirty clothes **detracted** from his appearance when interviewed.
The cyclist's concentration was *detracted* by hooligans and he collided with a car.	The cyclist's concentration was **distracted** by hooligans and he collided with a car.

71 – Device or Devise?

The noun **device** is a scheme, a plan, a contrivance, an emblem, an apparatus. The verb **to devise** means to contrive, to invent, or, as a legal term, to bequeath property in a Will.

Wrong	Corrected
The contract they offered insisted that work be completed by March 31st, ***a devise*** which tried to avoid allowances for the bad weather that often frustrates builders.	The contract they offered insisted that work be completed by March 31st, **a device** which tried to avoid allowances for the bad weather that often frustrates builders.
Edward has ***deviced*** a scheme to provide presents for all the old folk at Christmas.	Edward has **devised** a scheme to provide presents for all the old folk at Christmas.

72 – Diagnosis or Prognosis?

Use of **diagnosis** has extended beyond its original simple medical definition, which traces a disease by symptoms and appearance of the person examined. It is still basic in a doctor's language, but other problems in life and commerce are now **diagnosed.** "The surveyor eventually **diagnosed** the householder's problem as a slight subsidence in the property's foundations."

Prognosis, also a medical term, forecasts the course of a disease, and is now also written as a follow-up to other problems. "The surveyor gave the householder **a prognosis,** foretelling collapse of a house unless the repair of two walls was carried out within weeks."

Wrong	Corrected
The doctor examined little Geraldine and his ***prognosis*** was chicken-pox.	The doctor examined little Geraldine and his **diagnosis** was chicken-pox.
The car's engine stuttered but did not stop. However, it was the ***diagnosis*** of the disaster that was to follow in the mountains.	The car's engine stuttered but did not stop. However, it was the **prognosis** of the disaster that was to follow in the mountains.

73 – Different from or Different to?

Different from is Standard English. Old grammar manuals do not accept **different to.** Today **"That's different to** anything we've seen before" has won approval in places – but not here. Isn't a cabbage **different from** a cauliflower rather than ***different to*** it? Consider these basic meanings – **To** = in the direction of: **From** = separation.

Different than is not good English but is used, wrongly: "He writes stories **different than** those he wrote ten years ago".

Reported	Preferred
The book about grammar published in 1900 is ***different to*** the one on sale in Newcastle's bookshops.	The book about grammar published in 1900 is **different from** the one on sale in Newcastle's bookshops.
Johannesburg's traffic problems are a lot ***different to*** Birmingham's.	Johannesburg's traffic problems are a lot **different from** Birmingham's.

74 – Diffuse or Defuse?

Defuse is a verb that has recently become common. An explosive device becomes harmless when **the fuse is defused** – removed. The word has also taken on another meaning: **An argument is defused** when someone intervenes to settle it. In other words, the heat is taken out of the argument.

Diffuse, the verb, means to disperse, to shed, to spread. **Diffused,** the adjective = spread out, not concise. A man fails to succeed in business because his activities are **too diffuse** – he is involved in computers, golf clubs, clothing and printing.

Wrong	Corrected
Mediators from two churches ***diffused*** the anger over the quality of food served at the old people's home.	Mediators from two churches **defused** the anger over the quality of food served at the old people's home.
The sweet smell that henbane ***defuses*** suggests that the plant is poisonous.	The sweet smell that henbane **diffuses** suggests that the plant is poisonous.

75 – Disagree with or Disagree from?

Disagree with is correct. **"I shall disagree with him** over the value of the land he wants to buy." **Disagree** indicates a different opinion or stand. **"Disagreement with** the company's management is likely to lead to a strike by the two hundred workers."

Disagree from looks wrong in a sentence, sounds wrong in speech and is not acceptable here.

Wrong	Corrected
We disagree from the way your firm dealt with our complaint about the last delivery of footwear, which was below normal quality.	**We disagree with** the way your firm dealt with our complaint about the last delivery of footwear, which was below normal quality.

NOTE: We write **"agree to your proposal"** and **"agree with your opinion"**. *(See Agree with/agree to).*

76 – Disinterested or Uninterested ?

These words denote not interested broadly, but **disinterested** also has meanings unrelated to **uninterested.** The difference is often not recognised, leading to misuse of ***disinterested*** for **uninterested** – seldom the other way round.

Uninterested is not interested, maybe bored. **Not interested** is preferred, in speech. A keen student of computers may be **uninterested in agriculture.**

Disinterested means free from self-interest, acting with unselfish motives, without bias.

It is difficult to obtain **disinterested financial advice** from some companies because they are trying to sell their own insurance policies. Magistrates have to be interested in every word of evidence but their verdict should reflect **disinterest** in the people involved.

Wrong	Corrected
He is *disinterested* in his new job	He is **uninterested** (or not interested) in his new job.

77 – Disqualified or Unqualified?

Both **disqualified** and **unqualified** can be written as ineligible. But **disqualified** is normally the result of being banned, ruled out (a motorist convicted of driving when drunk may lose his licence). Anyone practising as a doctor must have passed examinations or he is **unqualified.**

Unqualified has another meaning in common use: **unqualified support** given to a political candidate is support without conditions or reservations.

Wrong	Corrected
The solicitor was sent to prison for five years, and he is certain to be *unqualified* from practising as a lawyer.	The solicitor was sent to prison for five years, and he is certain to be **disqualified** from practising as a lawyer.
A *disqualified* electrician is incapable of supervising other electricians.	An **unqualified** electrician is incapable of supervising other electricians.

78 – Draft or Draught?

A draft can be a document (e.g., a bank's authority for payment), an author's first thoughts for an article **drafted** on paper, or a military unit posted to a new location.

Draught, with the same pronunciation, is connected with drawing (by a **draughtsman),** drinking (a **draught** of ale), air and wind (a **draughty** passage) and the depth of water a ship needs. In some English-speaking countries, **draft** has completely replaced **draught. Draughts** is a popular board game.

Wrong	Corrected
It was a windy day and The *draft* blew away the *draught* of his article.	It was a windy day and the **draught** blew away the **draft** of his article.
We shall *draught* a contract for you to consider. Our *draftsman* has drawn a sketch of the layout	Wc shall **draft** a contract for you to consider. Our **draughtsman** has drawn a sketch of the layout

79 – Drank or Drunk? Sank or Sunk? Swam or Swum?

Inexcusable mistakes occur every day, even in educated circles, with the verbs **drink, sink** and **swim,** not in meaning but in tenses. Examples of errors (corrections in brackets):

I have drank **(drunk)** a pint.	*I drunk* **(drank)** two pints.
He sunk **(sank)** the putt.	That boat *has sank* **(sunk).**
They swum **(swam)** for an hour.	*I've swam* **(swum)** there.

The tenses are neither a puzzle nor ambiguous:

1 – **We drink** plenty of lemonade in our house.
2 – **We drank** lemonade instead of beer before lunch.
3 – **We have drunk** a gallon of lemonade since breakfast.

1 – **I sink** into depression when our son returns to Peru.
2 – **I sank** a bore-hole in the garden to find water.
3 – **I have sunk** all my spare money into property.

1 – **We swim** together six days every week.
2 – **We swam** across the bay yesterday morning.
3 – **We have swum** there many times before.

Wrong	Corrected
I *drunk* only water before driving to Edinburgh.	I **drank** only water before driving to Edinburgh.
If you *have drank* your coffee, we can go.	If you **have drunk** your coffee, we can go.
Judith *swum* the 100 metres in record time.	Judith **swam** the 100 metres in record time.
I have swam in that river.	**I have swum** in that river.
The ship *sunk* in three hundred metres of water.	The ship **sank** in three hundred metres of water.
Harold and Jim *have sank* more than twenty wells.	Harold and Jim **have sunk** more than twenty wells.

NOTE: Other verbs also create confusion. Examples (correct):

I sing	**ring**	**spring**	**stink**	**slink**	**fling**	**sting**	**string**	**run**
I sang	**rang**	**sprang**	**stank**	**slunk**	**flung**	**stung**	**strung**	**ran**
I have sung	**rung**	**sprung**	**stunk**	**slunk**	**flung**	**stung**	**strung**	**run**

Learning by Example

COMMON MISTAKES

Part three – E to I

80 – E.g., i.e., viz., sic

The first two abbreviations are in everyday use but are not always understood. One is sometimes written in error for the other. **E.g.** *(exempli gratia)* = for example. **I.e.** *(id est)* = that is.

Viz. *(videlicet)* = namely, that is to say. **Sic** is bracketed after an unusual phrase or a mistake to show that it was intended and not a printer's error.

> The Louvre, the national art gallery of France, has some of the world's outstanding paintings; **e.g.**, the Mona Lisa.
>
> We have so little space in our garden that we grow only the four vegetables needed most; **i.e.**, potatoes, cabbages, carrots and runner beans.
>
> The whole family were with us in the hotel on holiday; **viz.**, Arthur, William and Joan, the children, and their parents, Mr and Mrs Harrison.
>
> He wrote "You ought to be thrasht **(sic)** or sent to a remote prison, perhaps Dartmore **(sic)**".

81 – Either/Neither is (not are)

Either means one or the other of two. **Neither** means not either, not one, nor the other. Neither word is normally used when discussing more than two. **Any** is the word for **three or more.**

Traditional grammar: **"Either** (or **neither)** of the two will pay". Mistakes are common, spoken more often than written.

Grammatical problems arise when one noun or pronoun in a sentence is singular and the other is plural. We write **"They are or I am",** which perplexes us in such sentences as:

Either they or I AM responsible for the children's safety.

Although **am** relates to the subject **I,** it does not relate to the subject **they.** "Either they or I ***are responsible...***" is even less acceptable. When in doubt, re-write it: "Either they are responsible or I am".

Two singulars also mean problems: "Either he or I...**(am?)**".

Most grammar manuals now accept that the verb **(is** or **are** etc.) should agree with the nearest subject: "Either he or **I am paying**". But re-writing is an infallible solution:

Neither I nor you ARE fit enough to fly there tonight.

to be re-written as

Neither of us is fit enough to fly there tonight.
OR **Both of us are** unfit to fly there tonight.

Wrong	Corrected
Were either of the two boys responsible for the damage to your school?	**Was either** of the two boys responsible for the damage to your school?
Has either of the four men decided to work the overtime suggested?	**Has any one of the four** men decided to work the overtime suggested?
Neither of the many plans for a new industrial estate will be accepted.	**Not one** (or **none)** of the many plans for a new industrial estate will be accepted.
He made two suggestions, neither of which *meet* the company's need.	He made two suggestions, neither of which **meets** the company's need.

82 – Either is followed by OR Neither is followed by NOR

If **either** indicates a choice of two, **or** must follow and the verb must be singular if the subjects are singular: **"Either John or Charles knows** the road to Epping". With plural subjects a plural verb follows: **"Either** my children or my parents **know".**

Similarly, when **neither** is used to show an alternative, **nor** must follow. When the subjects are singular the verb is singular: **"Neither** my company **nor** yours **is** going to get that contract". Plural verb: **"Neither** the two cars **nor** the three lorries **are** to be sold".

When nouns or pronouns become linked and are singular and plural, the proximity rule is favoured: "Either my sons or **my brother is** coming".

Neither...or is a common mistake, even among well educated speakers who broadcast. ***Either...nor*** would be a unique error.

Wrong	Corrected
John and Joan have retired from the firm. ***Neither*** he ***or*** she ***have*** enjoyed good health in the past twelve months.	John and Joan have retired from the firm. **Neither** he **nor** she **has** enjoyed good health in the past twelve months.
Neither Ivy ***or*** Judy are well enough to travel with you.	**Neither** Ivy **nor** Judy is well enough to travel with you.
Neither the mansion ***or*** the cottage ***appeal*** to them.	**Neither** the mansion **nor** the cottage **appeals** to them.

The older grammar books are adamant that both **either...or** and **neither...nor** can apply to only one alternative – to two persons or things, not three. In other words, we should write **"Either** Ivy **or** Judy", but not ***"Either*** Ivy ***or*** Judy ***or*** Ethel". The theory still holds, although present-day practice accepts the following:

Either George, **or** Jim, **or** Edward will race today.
Neither George, **nor** Jim, **nor** Tom will race today.

Many – probably most – modern grammarians extend the licence to write "Either Sid **or** Tom **or** Alf **or** Ted will sing," but the preference here is:

We can promote Tom **or** George **or** Harold **or** Peter.

83 – Elder/Eldest or Older/Oldest?

Elder, as an adjective, **compares** the ages of **two** members of a family: "Joy is my **elder sister".** The superlative is **eldest:** "Joy's **eldest son** is Tom – he is the **tallest of the five".** Apart from family relationships, there are **elder statesmen.**

As nouns, **elder** and **eldest** are correct in "Joy is **the elder** of my sisters and Tom is **the eldest** of the children". **An elder** can also be an office-bearer in a church or a species of tree.

To compare the ages of other persons, groups or things, **older** is the word. It is the comparative of the adjective **old:** "Your father, at 57, is **five years older** than mine". The superlative is **oldest:** "He is the **oldest man** in Africa".

Wrong	Corrected
My *older sister* is a nun.	My **elder sister** is a nun.
He is almost 80 and is the *eldest man* there.	He is almost 80 and is the **oldest man** there.

84 – Emigrant or Immigrant or Migrant?

An **emigrant** leaves one country (say England) to settle in another (say Canada). He or she **emigrates.** Canada accepts that person, who has entered the country and intends to remain there, as an **immigrant.**

A migrant moves from one place of abode to another, not essentially from one country to another. Birds **migrate** from Siberia to spend the winter in parts of Europe.

Wrong	Corrected
They *immigrated* from Wales to New Zealand ten years ago and *immigrated* again last month to live in Canada.	They **emigrated** from Wales to New Zealand ten years ago and **emigrated** again last month to live in Canada.
Some *emigrants* sneaked into our country, which has such a vast coastline.	Some **immigrants** sneaked into our country, which has such a vast coastline.
Sharks *emigrate* from the Atlantic to the Pacific.	Sharks **migrate** from the Atlantic to the Pacific.

85 – Eminent or Imminent?

Pronunciation is close and meanings are occasionally reversed. **Eminent** is distinguished/exalted in its main use as an adjective. The Prime Minister of any country is usually an **eminent** person. **Imminent** means impending, about to happen. At five minutes to midnight on December 31st, the New Year is **imminent.**

Wrong	Corrected
The *eminent* arrival of the President of France will be greeted by at least 10,000 people at Victoria Station. It is some time since that country's most *imminent* person visited this country.	The **imminent** arrival of the President of France will be greeted by at least 10,000 people at Victoria Station. It is some time since that country's most **eminent** person visited this country.

86 – Enquire or Inquire?

Inquire and **inquiry** are gradually sweeping **enquire** and **enquiry** into the history books of word usage, although in the United Kingdom **enquire** is still seen often, with the same meaning.

Definitions taken from an old dictionary read: **Enquire** – To seek information. **Inquire** – To question, to investigate.

In those earlier times, to ask questions politely was **to enquire. Inquiry** (e.g., an inquest) was a thorough investigation. Such clear-cut meanings are accepted by many today. **"He enquired the price** of the chair" is common.

PREFERRED USES of Enquire, enquiry...Inquire, inquiry
I **enquired** at the council offices where the public **inquiry** into the Compit planning application will be held next month. The Government has appointed a High Court judge to **inquire** into the cause of the railway disaster. My **enquiry** at the post office provided the information about the postal rates for Christmas cards to be sent abroad. He **inquired** (or **enquired**) at the police station about the watch he lost at the fairground last week.

87 – Envelop or Envelope?

Pronunciation determines the right word. **Envelop,** the verb, induces the weight of the voice on **-vel-.** The word indicates that we are going to wrap something round an object – to surround it, to envelop it.

Envelope, the noun, is the casing into which a letter is placed, The emphatic syllables are **en-** and **-lope.**

Wrong	Corrected
I've written the letter. Pass me an *envelop,* please.	I've written the letter. Pass me an **envelope,** please.
Weeds now *envelope* the flowers in our front garden.	Weeds now **envelop** the flowers in our front garden.

88 – Every / Everyone / Everybody IS

Every means each. **Body** is one person. Singular nouns and verbs, follow all three. **Every one** may refer to things but **everyone** is synonymous with **everybody** and cannot be used for things.

Every woman in the village **is** trying to become a non-smoker.

Everyone **hopes** to win something from the football pools.

Every one of the cottages **needs** a new roof before winter.

Wrong	Corrected
Everybody who *take* part *have* a chance to win a fortune in the competition.	**Everybody** who **takes** part **has** a chance to win a fortune in the competition.
Every runner in the marathon *have* a medal to show that *they finished the course.*	**Every** runner in the marathon **has** a medal to show that **he or she finished the course.**

Problem 1 – "**Everyone** here must make **his** own bed". General advice allows **his** also to represent **her,** but a better alternative is "All of you here must make your own beds".

Problem 2 – "Pay **every** worker before they **leave** tonight". The alternative: "Pay **all workers** before they leave tonight".

89 – Explicit or Implicit?

An **explicit** statement is clear, plainly expressed, definite, with no likelihood of misunderstanding. "Get out of this shop" is an **explicit** instruction.

Implicit is close in meaning. Implicit instructions are to be understood, although not specifically stated: "Stuart Catchpole and Bob Shaw signed no formal contract but there was an **implicit understanding** that they would work amicably together in restoring the old barn".

Wrong	Corrected
I told Mr Gerard Thomas that we were willing to pay £800 for a second consignment of batteries. I took it as ***explicit*** acceptance of the price, because he said nothing about it; he went on to discuss delivery dates.	I told Mr Gerard Thomas that we were willing to pay £800 for a second consignment of batteries. I took it as **implicit** acceptance of the price, because he said nothing about it; he went on to discuss delivery dates.
Sid said: "Turn right into Church Street, then left into Paul's Lane – our house is the first on the left". His directions were ***implicit.***	Sid said: "Turn right into Church Street, then left into Paul's Lane – our house is the first on the left". His directions were **explicit.**

90 – Extrovert or Introvert?

They are opposites – antonyms. **An extrovert** may be an exhibitionist with a strong personality and few reservations in social behaviour, without misbehaving badly.

An introvert is probably shy, possibly self-centred and not given to apparent emotions, although he or she may suffer much worry and fear inwardly.

Wrong	Corrected
Albert threw a party, danced on the table playing a tambourine and sang about his brilliance as a comedian. He is ***an introvert.***	Albert threw a party, danced on the table playing a tambourine and sang about his brilliance as a comedian. He is **an extrovert.**

91 – First or Firstly? Second or Secondly? Third or Thirdly?

As adjectives: **The first** (or the **second,** or the **third) choice** will be Durban for this year's holiday.

As adverbs: **First,** we were told that the piano would not be delivered today; **second,** we were told it would be next week; **third,** we were told that the price had increased.

When **-ly** is added *(adverbs):* **Firstly,** the quickest way to London from Rome is by air. **Secondly,** hotels in inner London are more expensive than those in the suburbs. **Thirdly,** a week at least is needed to visit the Tower of London, Hampton Court and the other historic sights.

We can take away doubts. Any of them may be used. But the preference is to write or say "**First,** let me tell you..." and then "**Secondly/thirdly,** let me tell you...".

92 – Foreign Words: Are they needed?

Many foreign words have become absorbed into the English language. Most are French or Latin; a few are Greek. Dictionaries define some words as English without reference to their origins. Examples from the French:

abattoir **chassis** **chauffeur** **bouquet**

Others have been adopted because they express a fact, an act, or a feeling more succinctly than any English word. Examples:

cul de sac *(a road or path without an outlet)*

ad infinitum *(without end)* **bona fide** *(genuine)*

sine die *(day or date not named when decision postponed)*

sub judice *(criminal charge or case under consideration)*

magnum opus *(lifetime's greatest work, usually literary)*

pro rata *(in proportion to another figure)*

fait accompli *(an accomplished deed)*

status quo *(unaltered condition)* **faux pax** *(social mistake)*

Foreign words are sometimes used unnecessarily, perhaps to demonstrate superior education. Why, for instance, replace "time flies" with *tempus fugit,* or "double meaning" with *double entendre,* or "between ourselves" with *entre nous?*

93 – Formally or Formerly?

Formerly and **formally** *(adverbs)* are confusable, particularly in speech. Few mistakes are made with the adjectives, **formal** and **former.**

Formerly refers to an occurrence before the present time, previously. **Formally** indicates an act that was conducted, executed or performed according to regulations or tradition. Use of **former** and **formal** is illustrated in this sentence:

> Mr. Smith, **former principal** of St. Ina's College and **formerly** headmaster of my school, was installed as vice-chancellor of the university in a **formal ceremony** yesterday.

Wrong	Corrected
Formally they were the best team in East Africa, with a *formal* international player as coach.	**Formerly** they were the best team in East Africa, with a **former** international player as coach.
He was *formerly* elected as the town's mayor yesterday.	He was **formally** elected as the town's mayor yesterday.

94 – Founder or Flounder?

These verbs produce much uncertainty, probably because they are not in common use. **To founder** refers mainly to a sinking ship or to fail. A horse that becomes lame **founders.** So does a building that falls down. **To flounder** is to stumble or struggle, as might a drunkard.

Wrong	Corrected
The boat floundered just as they reached the man who was already unconscious in the stormy sea.	**The boat foundered** just as they reached the man who was already unconscious in the stormy sea.
We have seen that young man, who has inherited a fortune, *foundering about the town* for weeks, late at night and usually drunk. He told me "My life has *floundered* in an ocean of alcohol".	We have seen that young man, who has inherited a fortune, **floundering about the town** for weeks, late at night and usually drunk. He told me "My life has **foundered** in an ocean of alcohol".

95 – Further or Farther?

1 – There is little consistency in the use of **further** and **farther.** Winston Churchill insisted that, in matters of distance, **farther** was correct. That is the preference here.

Further has a wider definition than **farther,** with a basic meaning of "in addition to". It may be unpopular to say that it should not refer to distance, because the majority will contend that "Look for it in a **further corner of the room"** is as correct as "Look for it in a **farther corner of the room**".

"You will find the football ground **farther** down the road" is preferred to *"further* down the road", although "about two miles down the road" would be better than either, if the distance is known. *(The best reports, memoranda and letters include precise rather than vague information.)* **Farther,** written alone, will always be indefinite, except when the statement is similar to "He pointed to the **farther** house".

The superlative **farthest** can be definite: "The **farthest** he will travel in one day is 250 miles".

2 – When time and reasoning are reported or discussed and the meaning is **more** rather than distance, the correct word is **further.**

We will not discuss the plan **further** today.

Further, no worker will receive a salary increase or bonus this year, because the firm has lost a lot of money.

The city's central library is shut until **further notice.**

Reported	Preferred
We shall set out from Hayle on Wednesday, but we cannot expect to cycle *further* than Exeter in one day.	We shall set out from Hayle on Wednesday, but we cannot expect to cycle **farther** than Exeter in one day.
The *furthest* point East in England is Lowestoft.	The **farthest** point East in England is Lowestoft.
I don't wish to discuss the subject *farther.*	I don't wish to discuss the subject **further.**

GRAMMATICAL NOTE: **Farther** and **further** above are adjectives or adverbs. **Further** can be a verb: **"To further** his career, he is taking a course in electronics".

96 – To get / I got / They have got

The verb **to get** has meanings that stretch from to obtain (a job), to win (a prize), to suffer (an injury) and to reach (a place after a journey).

Get and **got** are among the most colloquially-used words in the English language, often in place of a more descriptive verb. They are seen and heard needlessly more often than most.

Reported	Preferred
They have ***got*** a pig to sell.	They **have** a pig to sell.
He has ***got*** first prize.	He has **won** first prize.
I ***got*** tired on the journey, and by the time we ***got*** to London I hadn't ***got*** the energy to ***get*** to Chelsea to see the match. So I ***got*** into bed.	I grew tired on the journey, and when we **reached** London I **hadn't** the energy **to go** to Chelsea to see the match. So I **went** to bed.
The car went off the road and hit a tree, and all three men in it ***got*** killed.	The car went off the road and hit a tree, and all three men in it **were** killed.
Go and get yourself washed, before your father ***gets*** home from the factory.	Go and wash, before your father **comes** home from the factory.
She wrecked the manager's car and was lucky not ***to get*** sacked.	She wrecked the manager's car and was lucky not **to be** sacked.

In speech, **get** and **got** fall naturally from the tongue and are not always to be dismissed as errors or unacceptable. They are not easily replaceable sometimes as in **"Get ready. Get dressed"**. Other examples where meanings are clear:

I got a black eye	– *refers to a past point of time.*
I had got a black eye	– *tells of a past condition.*
She has got to see the doctor	– *says she must or needs to see the doctor.*
She has to see the doctor	– *implies a commitment to see the doctor.*
They got engaged	– *suggests a happening, an event.*

97 – Hackneyed phrases (Clichés)

Hackneyed phrases are known as clichés (French, *translated as stereotype*). The argument against them is that readers and listeners become tired of them. ***"Meaningful talks around the negotiating table"*** is one example.

At an inquiry, a senior servant was not prepared to say that someone's statement was a lie. He shaded his criticism into **"economical with the truth"**. That was accepted immediately in everyday speech and in print as novel and brilliant, and must now be classed as a cliché.

A consensus of opinions rates these as stale phrases:

Conspicuous by its absence. **At this moment in time.**

In this day and age. **Over the moon.**

Space of time. **Food for thought.**

It's on our agenda. **Warts and all.** **Sour grapes.**

Meaningful talks around the negotiating table.

Bored to tears. **Tongue in cheek.**

Explore every avenue. **Green with envy.**

In the pink of condition. **Taste of his own medicine.**

Snatch victory from the jaws of defeat.

Wild goose chase. **Sick as a parrot.**

Last but not least. **It's not my cup of tea.**

Six of one and half a dozen of the other.

As cool as a cucumber. **Back to square one.**

Clichés, however, are not outlawed, and are preferable to the jargon written in many official and legal documents. A cliché can often be more effective than a phrase a writer or speaker composes in haste. Their use is a matter of personal choice. Most are created by journalists and writers of scripts for radio and television.

Some in constant use can be found in the classics. **"More in sorrow than in anger"** has been dubbed a cliché, yet it is a quotation from Shakespeare.

"I can see a light at the end of the tunnel" would be regarded as a cliché. But a TV script writer gave us ***"He could see a light at the end of the tunnel* – it was a train coming to meet him"**. That was a profound expression of a disaster to follow.

98 – Half or Halve?

Mistakes – they are common – result from confusing the verb **halve** with the noun, adjective or adverb **half.**

A half *(noun)* is one of two equal parts into which anything is or may be divided. "I have a pumpkin. Pass me your knife – **I will cut a half for you.**" The plural: **halves.**

Half *(adjective)* denotes half a standard value: "We are selling it **half price**".

Half *(Adverb)* indicates the degree or extent of a half. "It was a **journey half completed.**"

To halve *(verb)* is to divide something into two equal parts.

Wrong	Corrected
Your bank overdraft may be a worry, but you could ***half it*** by selling your antiques.	Your bank overdraft may be a worry, but you could **halve it** by selling your antiques.

99 – Hanged or Hung?

Hanged refers to the hanging of a convicted prisoner or other unfortunate person. Example:

> Seven men were **hanged** in Far Eastern countries last year for drug smuggling. Another man hanged himself.

Hung is used in all other cases. "I **hung/have hung** the pictures in the gallery."

Wrong	Corrected
Dr Crippen was ***hung*** at Pentonville in 1910, and notice of the execution was ***hanged*** on the prison door. He had murdered his wife. He was hanging around to borrow my tools, but hc ***hanged on*** to them too long last year, so I refused to lend them this time.	Dr Crippen was **hanged** at Pentonville in 1910, and notice of the execution was **hung on** the prison door. He had murdered his wife. He was hanging around to borrow my tools, but he **hung on** to them too long last year, so I refused to lend them this time.

100 – Idle or Idol or Idyll?

An idle person is doing nothing, or as little as possible. The description usually extends critically to the lazy or useless.

An idol is an image that is worshipped. Many entertainers, sportsmen and sportswomen also **become idols to their fans.** Anyone **idolized** is loved and honoured.

An idyll is a short poem about a picturesque country scene. More commonly written is the adjective **idyllic,** describing a lovely setting, even a lovely life.

Wrong	Corrected
No one could be more *idol* than the young man who inherited £3 million when his aunt died last year.	No one could be more **idle** than the young man who inherited £3 million when his aunt died last year.
The *idle* of last night's pop concert was Cliff Richard.	The **idol** of last night's pop concert was Cliff Richard.

101 – Illegible or Eligible?

Confusion is not common but it does occur, mainly in speech. **Eligible** means qualified. **Ineligible** means not qualified. Young people reach an age when they are **eligible** to drive a car. **Illegible** describes handwriting or print as unreadable. **Legible** writing is clear enough to be read.

Wrong	Corrected
Are you *illegible* for next week's race?	Are you **ineligible** for next week's race?
Ted is the most *legible* bachelor in our street.	Ted is the most **eligible** bachelor in our street.
Eligible writing makes the essay *illegible* for a prize.	**Illegible** writing makes the essay **ineligible** for a prize.
If Mary's shorthand notes are not clearly *eligible,* an accurate transcription is unlikely.	If Mary's shorthand notes are not clearly **legible,** an accurate transcription is unlikely.

102 – Illicit or Elicit?

Misunderstandings are mainly in speech, pronunciation being similar. Meanings are completely different. **Illicit** *(adjective)* describes something that is happening. **An illicit act** is against the law or regulations. **Elicit** *(verb)* does something.

There may be **illicit drinking** of alcohol in an unlicensed club. A detective's questions will try to **elicit** (draw out) **information** from a person suspected of an offence.

Wrong	Corrected
Neighbours believe that Mr A is seeing Mrs B in an *elicit* affair.	Neighbours believe that Mr A is seeing Mrs B in an **illicit** affair.
If you can *illicit* the facts, the police will act against the man you say is selling you stolen beef.	If you can **elicit** the facts, the police will act against the man you say is selling you stolen beef.

103 – Impel or Compel?

To compel is to bring about a result by force, verbal or physical. **To impel** is to induce or to persuade; to be impelled can be a natural instinct.

A person compelled to pay a tax levied by the government has no alternative. **To be impelled to help** an old lady across the road may come from an inward feeling of moral obligation.

Wrong	Corrected
A guilty conscience *compelled* me to apologise to my neighbour for the harsh words I shouted at him over the fence about his dog.	A guilty conscience **impelled** me to apologise to my neighbour for the harsh words I shouted at him over the fence about his dog.
There are *impelling* reasons under a local by-law to protect the public from the dangers a hidden mineshaft creates.	There are **compelling** reasons under a local by-law to protect the public from the dangers a hidden mineshaft creates.

104 – Imply or Infer?

To imply is to suggest indirectly something that was not actually said. It can be an insinuation. **To infer** is to draw conclusions or to interpret the meaning of what has been said or written. **If you imply,** you write or say something. **If you infer,** you read it or hear it. Confusion is common.

Letters in newspapers implied that a travel agent exaggerated the facilities a holiday hotel provided. **Readers inferred** that the holidaymakers were dissatisfied and angry.

Wrong	Corrected
They infer in their letter that you have no case to justify a reduction in the rent for your house.	**They imply** in their letter that you have no case to justify a reduction in the rent for your house.
From what the manager said, *I implied* that he would drop me for the next match.	From what the manager said, **I inferred** that he would drop me for the next match.
Your letter stated that we must place an order at once, *inferring* that stocks were low and that the price will rise next month.	Your letter stated that we must place an order at once, **implying** that stocks were low and that the price will rise next month.

105 – Inability or Disability?

Disability is almost always associated with a physical or mental handicap. Both incapacities are seen in: "His **disabilities** as a writer of letters were apparent in one he sent to the editor of his local newspaper".

Inability means being unable to do something. That could be inability to drive a car or inability to think clearly after a serious road accident.

Wrong	Corrected
My *disability* to drive your car results from the awful *inability* I suffered in the battle at Arnhem.	My **inability** to drive your car results from the awful **disability** I suffered in the battle at Arnhem.

106 – Incite or Insight?

To incite is to urge, provoke, tempt or excite someone into action. **Incitement** *(noun)* **to disaffection** is the serious wartime offence of persuading a soldier not to fight.

Insight is a searching look into a problem, discernment, a clear perception, intuition.

Wrong	Corrected
The *incite* of a psychiatrist is needed if reasons behind the murder of those three children by the father are to be found. Something must have *insighted* him.	The **insight** of a psychiatrist is needed if reasons behind the murder of those three children by the father is to be found. Something must have **incited** him.

107 – Incomparable or Uncomparable?

They are not interchangeable; they are introduced here only because some writers are confused into using the rare word *uncomparable* for **incomparable.** Misspelling gives the wrong meaning.

Incomparable means matchless, unequalled, unrivalled, second to none, supreme, greatest.

Uncomparable means not capable of being compared. The income of a millionaire cannot be compared with that of a farm worker.

Wrong	Corrected
It was an *uncomparable* achievement for Tom to win five cups at this year's horticultural show. The best in any previous year was two won by his brother Sid. Young Harold said: "The *most superlative essay* I wrote last term was about a storm". Harold forgot that the word superlative is *incomparable*.	It was an **incomparable** achievement for Tom to win five cups at this year's horticultural show. The best in any previous year was two won by his brother Sid. Young Harold wrote: "The *most superlative essay* I wrote last term was about a storm". Harold forgot that the word superlative is **uncomparable**.

108 – Inflict or Afflict?

To inflict is to impose pain or punishment on someone. "It was wrong to **inflict** a prison sentence on him." Noun: **infliction.**

To afflict is to cause pain, distress or sorrow. "He has been **afflicted** with asthma for ten years." Noun: **affliction.**

Wrong	Corrected
Those hooligans *afflicted* frightful injuries on an old man who has been *inflicted* with a spinal deformity since birth.	Those hooligans **inflicted** frightful injuries on an old man who has been **afflicted** with a spinal deformity since birth.
Affliction of an extra £400 in tax is crippling for us.	**Infliction** of an extra £400 in tax is crippling for us.

109 – Insure or Ensure or Assure?

The meaning of each word is suggested in this sentence: **"Insure** with a good company to cover all possible misfortunes before flying to Asia, **ensure** that loss of important documents is included and **assure** your wife that she has no reason to worry".

To ensure is to make certain and secure (making sure there is enough time to catch the train and that your house is secure).

To insure ensures that, if a car is stolen, the insurance company will provide money to replace it. Noun: **insurance.**

To assure gives confidence to someone that all will be well. "Hold my hand; you will not fall." Noun: **assurance.**

Wrong	Corrected
Our house is *ensured* for £150,000, with an *assurance policy* mainly to cover fire risks	Our house is **insured** for £150,000, with an **insurance policy** mainly to cover fire risks
A bank loan *insures* that the house can be repaired. I was *ensured* that the offer would be confirmed.	A bank loan **ensures** that the house can be repaired. I was **assured** that the offer would be confirmed.

110 – Interval or Interlude?

The difference is minor. **Interval** can be a pause, a break between two happenings or two events. The audience often disperses. Lamp-posts are placed at regular **intervals.**

Interlude is also an interval, during which there is a minor performance that is different from the main event.

Reported	Correct
The interval at the symphony concert was a fascinating dancing display.	**The interlude** at the symphony concert was a fascinating dancing display.
Interludes between races were long, and there was little to occupy us. We went home.	**Intervals** between races were long, and there was little to occupy us. We went home.

111 – Into or In to?

Errors are common. The question when deciding the use of **into** or **in to** is: To which word or words is **to** attached? Examples:

They are calling you **in** | | **to** see the chairman.

George, you're next **in** | | **to** bat.

How did you get yourself | | **into** that mess?

They are calling you | | **into** the room.

Wrong	Corrected
I saw the car crash *in to* the stationary lorry.	I saw the car crash **into** the stationary lorry.
He had broken *in to* the shoe factory and then *went into see* if there was a safe in the office.	He had broken **into** the shoe factory and then **went in to see** if there was a safe in the office.
He went into find all of them asleep in the kitchen.	**He went in to find** all of them asleep in the kitchen.
He forced his way *into claim* a seat on the train.	He forced his way **in to claim** a seat on the train.

112 — -Ise or -Ize ending of words? Realize or Realise?

Should we write **realize** or **realise, criticize** or **criticise, itemize** or **itemise?** Opinion is divided. Most grammarians, including those responsible for much of the output from specialist publishing houses, use **-ize** where they find clear evidence in the history of a particular word. But almost all the popular press in the United Kingdom, with a readership of 20 million or more, prefers **-ise.**

The choice here is **-ise,** because the author's working life has been much longer in journalism than in further education. He has to concede, however, that the pronunciation in most cases is **-ize** and that almost all the dictionaries he consulted recorded **itemize** and **realize,** although the latest *Concise Oxford Dictionary* adds **or -ise** in many cases.

Advice: Make your own decision and be consistent. Do not write ***realize*** in one sentence and ***itemise*** in another.

Common words written to end in either **-ize** or **-ise** include the following:

liquidize **or liquidise**	***crystallize*** **or crystallise**
sympathize **or sympathise**	***privatize*** **or privatise**
dramatize **or dramatise**	***organize*** **or organise**
immunize **or immunise**	***apologize*** **or apologise**
modernize **or modernise**	***sterilize*** **or sterilise**
civilize **or civilise**	***baptize*** **or baptise**
recognize **or recognise**	***jeopardize*** **or jeopardise**
finalize **or finalise**	***pulverize*** **or pulverise**
authorize **or authorise**	***minimize*** **or minimise**

While the alternative exists for those above and many more, several are accepted as ending in **-ise** only. Examples:

advertise	**supervise**	**advise**	**devise**
comprise	**exercise**	**arise**	**despise**
improvise	**revise**	**televise**	**chastise**
surprise	**surmise**	**uprise**	**enterprise**

The uncertainties make a good case for **-ise** endings only. In the eyes of most of us, mistakes would then be avoided. It is also an aspect of our language which an English Language Authority *(see The Last Word, pages 178, 179)* might discuss and provide recommendations for, conscious of the fact, perhaps, that **-ize** predominates in the United States.

113 – It is I or It is me?

In formal English **It is I** is grammatically correct and ***It is me*** is said to be colloquial, because the pronoun that follows the verb **to be** should be in the subjective *(see page 19)* form:

It is we (not *It is us*).	**It is he (not *It is him*).**
It is she (not *It is her*).	**It is they (not *It is them*).**

In education that rule was rigid until about 40 years ago, but most examiners now accept ***It is me*** without penalty, unless the question has been set specifically for discussion in that area of grammar. **It is I,** of course, could not be classed as wrong. And where the pronoun is the subject of a verb, the regular form would be used: **"It was she** who broke the glass".

When spoken as exclamations, **It's me!** (pointing a finger at himself or herself) and **It's him!** (pointing at someone) must be accepted even by those who refuse to break with tradition.

The best advice may be to recognise **It is I** as correct but to find an alternative phrase if one wishes to sidestep it, as in:

Jones has resigned. **It is he** who must face the consequences.

Re-written –

Jones has resigned. **He** must face the consequences.

Doubts on **I/me, he/him, she/her, we/us, they/them** can usually be cleared by adding or deleting words. Examples:

A taxi will take ***Jean and I*** to the Derby – WRONG.
A taxi will take *(delete Jean and)* me to the Derby – RIGHT.

Who broke the gate? ***Them*** – WRONG.
Who broke the gate? They did *(broke it)* – RIGHT.

Colloquial	Correct
Only ***you and me*** will be able to find the house.	Only **you and** I will be able to find the house.
The manager blames ***you and I*** for the fall in profits.	The manager blames **you and me** for the fall in profits.
Yes, ***it was me*** who posted the letter.	Yes, **it was I** who posted the letter.
Me and John will join you at the church service.	**John and I** will join you at the church service.

114 – It's senseless MY smoking – right / It's senseless ME smoking – wrong

This is another case where correct grammar is disregarded deliberately or ignorantly because it is claimed that **my** for ***me*** in some of its uses jars the senses.

The general use of **my, his, her, its, our, your** and **their** has no problem. They are better described as possessive adjectives, not personal pronouns – "Hand me **my** dictionary". They slip off the tongue naturally. Mistakes occur when they are linked to words ending in **-ing.**

Write is a verb: "He **writes** to me". **Writing** is the present participle of that verb: **"I am writing** to John tomorrow". And **writing** can also be a verbal noun: "I think highly of **his writing** to you at this difficult time". *(Present participle, see page 14. Verbal noun, page 2).*

Note that **in front of the verbal noun writing** we use **his,** a possessive adjective, and not the personal pronoun ***him.*** We apply that rule as follows – **My,** not ***me:*** **his,** not ***him:*** **her,** and **her: its,** not ***it:*** your, not ***you:*** their, not ***them.***

The logic of this corner of English grammar is seen when two sentences are analysed for meaning:

> I detest ***him*** painting that door red and purple – WRONG.
> I detest **his** painting that door red and purple – RIGHT.

The first sentence detests the man. The second detests the colours. Another example:

> I followed ***them*** jumping at yesterday's gymkhana – WRONG.

He was not on a horse jumping the fences and following them but was one of the spectators watching **their jumping.**

Wrong	Corrected
What's the use ***him waiting.***	What's the use **his waiting.**
Excuse ***me not visiting*** her.	Excuse **my not visiting** her.
It's good ***them coming*** early.	It is good **their coming** early.
Imagine ***us winning*** that million pounds!	Imagine **our winning** that million pounds!

NOTE: "I saw **him waiting". "**Don't keep **us waiting."** Correct.

115 – Tim and myself played today – wrong

Tim and I played today – right

He hurt himself when he fell – right

You yourself broke it – right

Don't be intimidated by the grammatical term reflexive pronoun. **Myself, yourself, himself, herself, itself, ourselves, yourselves** and **themselves** are self-explanatory. Looking in a mirror, you see a reflection of yourself. When writing a phrase, the use of **myself** or one of the other seven is a reflection of **I, you, he, she, it, we, you** or **they.**

> I see **myself** as Romeo in the school play. The producers, however, will please **themselves.**

A second use for reflexive pronouns describes them in some grammar books as EMPHATIC. They emphasise the pronoun or noun:

> Jim blamed Harold but he **himself** cracked the jug.

Mistakes are few but in some cases unacceptable may be more appropriate than wrong. Before using one, check whether **I, me,** or any of the other personal pronouns would read better.

Unacceptable or disliked	Correct
He owed the money to *Albert and myself.*	He owed the money to **Albert and me.**
She and himself left today.	**She and he** left today.
Your father and yourself are welcome.	**Your father and you** are welcome.
If it is up to myself, there will be no carnival in Halt.	**If it is up to me,** there will be no carnival in Halt.
Wrong	**Correct**
They think *theirselves* lucky to be alive after that flood.	They think **themselves** lucky to be alive after that flood.

NOTE: Mistakes are rare with possessive pronouns – **mine, his, hers, ours, yours** and **theirs** are used in these examples:

> That boat of **yours** is worth nothing.
>
> This car is **mine.**

116 – It's or Its?

It's is an abbreviation of **It is** or **It has.** Mistakes are many, probably the most common in the English language. Yet no one above the age of ten should be confused in their use – their meanings are vastly different.

Evidence of the carelessness and ignorance that exist was seen in an important organisation's advertisement in a quality English newspaper which printed *it's* for **its** three times in two sentences *(*** See them in Wrong/Corrected below).*

Its indicates possession of something. Understanding its use is easy, provided possession is remembered. Examples:

> Bert Brown has moved into his new house. **It's** *(it is)* time he cleaned **its** *(the house's)* windows.
>
> Where is your little Fido? **It's** *(it is)* time we saw to **its** *(the dog's)* dinner.

Wrong	Corrected
*** Prove ***it's democratic nature*** by allowing any of ***it's members*** who wish to do so to leave.	Prove **its democratic nature** by allowing any of **its members** who wish to do so to leave.
*** No movement which needs force to maintain the allegiance of ***it's members*** can be taken seriously.	No movement which needs force to maintain the allegiance of **its members** can be taken seriously.
His new car is up to ***it's bumpers*** in flood water.	His new car is up to **its bumpers** in flood water.
We trust no one now, and believe nothing unless ***its in black and white.***	We trust no one now, and believe nothing unless **it's in black and white.**
Its useless protesting. Your van was parked there an hour over ***it's*** time.	**It's useless** protesting. Your van was parked there an hour over **its** time.
Pass that book. ***Its the one*** I've been looking for.	Pass that book. **It's the one** I've been looking for.
Its a pity you were away.	**It's a pity** you were away.

Test use of **its** by replacing it with **your, his, her** or **their.**

Learning by Example

COMMON MISTAKES

Part four – J to Q

117 – Judicial or Judicious? Adjudicate

Judicial is pertinent to the courts of justice, to judges and administration of the law. The **judiciary** are the judges.

Judicious reflects sound judgment, which will be wise, prudent and sensible. **To adjudicate** is to try (in the sense of test) and decide, to pronounce judgment, to preside as judge at a contest unconnected with the law. It could be a beauty competition or judging carrots at the local horticultural show.

Reported	Corrected
Mary sought maintenance from her husband at a *judicious* hearing before magistrates, who accepted her evidence as *judicial* and sincere.	Mary sought maintenance from her husband at a **judicial** hearing before magistrates, who accepted her evidence as **judicious** and sincere.

118 – To lay or To lie?

These two verbs cause much confusion. An examination question produces many answers that do not conform to the following:

I lie	on my bed thinking of our problems.
I lay	in the sunshine yesterday till it became unbearable.
I have lain	for hours on the beach.
I lay	the cloth on the table just like this.
I laid	the books on the floor because the shelves were full.
I have laid	four pumpkins on the grass for your wife to see.
I lie	about my age to men, as I am lying to you now.
I lied	to the police, as you **have lied** to them so often.

To lie means to be in a horizontal position. It is an intransitive verb **(I lie comfortably** – the action remains with the performer; there is no object).

To lie can also mean to tell a falsehood.

To lay means to place something, to put it down in some order, to spread it on a surface. It is a transitive verb and an object follows **(I lay the bricks)**.

Wrong	Corrected
He lies when he tells you that *I laid on the beach* in the nude.	He lies when he tells you that **I lay on the beach** in the nude.
I saw your book. *It was laying on the desk* in George's office. *I am not lieing to you.*	I saw your book. **It was lying on the desk** in George's office. **I am not lying to you.**
I lay here every day after lunch.	**I lie here** every day after lunch.

NOTE: "I lay here every day" is correct if it was in the past that I lay there.

Wrong	Corrected
I have lain your shirts on your bed in the next room.	**I have laid your shirts on your bed** in the next room.
The President *lay the* foundation *stone.*	The President **laid the** foundation **stone.**
The statesman's body *will lay in state* till tomorrow.	The statesman's body **will lie in state** till tomorrow.

119 — Lawyers: Barrister or solicitor?

Lawyer is a term used for **barrister** or **solicitor,** titles that are assumed only after difficult examinations have been passed. Many people not familiar with the legal system are confused over the respective qualifications and duties.

A solicitor gives legal advice to clients and may represent them in the lower courts — mainly magistrates' courts — although there are now conditions in which they can appear before judges in the higher courts. A solicitor's work, however, is largely counselling clients face-to-face, or writing to them, and preparing documents such as those needed by businesses, for Wills and for the conveyance of property.

A barrister (known as **an advocate in Scotland**) acts as adviser to clients on specialist legal matters when briefed by a solicitor and can represent them in any court, usually the High Court or Court of Appeal. On the recommendation of the Lord Chancellor, a barrister may be elevated to the rank of Queen's Counsel (taking silk — wearing a silk gown) and, ultimately, he or she may become a judge.

Wrong	Corrected
We have authorised *the barrister* to instruct a good *solicitor* to appear for our son in the Court of Appeal.	We have authorised **the solicitor** to instruct a good **barrister** to appear for our son in the Court of Appeal.

120 — Lead or Led?

To lead has several meanings, the most common being in front in competition, in conducting, in showing the way. Mistakes occur in past tenses **(I led, I have led),** with *lead* written for **led.**

The main reason for misspelling is the identical pronunciation in past tenses. We say "I was **led** to believe that the parcel was light but I found it to be as heavy as a lump of **lead**".

Wrong	Corrected
I shall show you the way over the mountains and take the route *your brother lead his party* last year.	I shall show you the way over the mountains and take the route **your brother led his party** last year.

121 – Learn or Teach?

Learn is sometimes wrongly written for **teach. To learn** is to receive knowledge, not only within the educational system but from experience gained in a craft or duty in house or workplace. Experience is a process of learning.

To teach is to instruct, to impart knowledge, to educate. Teaching may be in school, college, in the home or in the factory.

Wrong	Corrected
I will try to ***learn you how to write*** applications for lecturing jobs in Australia.	I will try to **teach you how to write** applications for lecturing jobs in Australia.

The past tense and past participle can be **learned** or **learnt. Learned** is also an adjective, heard every day in the courts of justice, where a lawyer is referred to as "my **learned** friend". In this case, the pronunciation is different – "my **learn-ed** friend", spoken with two distinct syllables.

122 – Lease or Lessee or Lessor?

A lease is a contract, usually drawn up by a lawyer, hiring property to a tenant for a fixed time. The owner is **the lessor** and the tenant is **the lessee.**

A new word, **lease-back,** has come into the British business vocabulary – the owner sells his building or land to another party and continues to occupy it as **a lessee** paying rent.

It probably evolved from **lend-lease,** the term given to an Act introduced by President Roosevelt in 1941 enabling Congress to lend or lease defence equipment and services to any country important to the defence of the United States.

Wrong	Corrected
The lessee decided not to renew the lease on the shop after 21 years because ***the lessor*** had always been late in paying the rent and was now a year in arrears.	**The lessor** decided not to renew the lease on the shop after 21 years because **the lessee** had always been late in paying the rent and was now a year in arrears.

123 – Less or Fewer?

Less relates to quantity in bulk and achievement **(less coal, less skill). Fewer** refers to numbers **(fewer students, fewer votes).** The general rule is **fewer** with plural nouns and **less** with nouns that have no plural form.

Less is constantly spoken and written instead of **fewer.** It is not good English. There are exceptions. We would write "He was **less than** five metres away" and not ***"Fewer than",*** as the words imply a single unit of distance. Similarly, "He ran the marathon in **less than three hours".**

Wrong	Corrected
There will be *less opportunities* for your skills in South America.	There will be **fewer opportunities** for your skills in South America.
The number of spectators at the show today was *less* than yesterday's record.	The number of spectators at the show today was **smaller** than yesterday's record.
NOTE: Smaller for fewer is a preference rather than a correction.	
The takings were fewer because there were *less people* at the exhibition.	**The takings were less** because there were **fewer people** at the exhibition.

124 – Libel or Slander?

Libel is a defamatory statement published or broadcast. **Slander** is spoken defamation, except on radio and television, which have been brought within the law of libel in the United Kingdom because their audiences are extensive.

Wrong	Corrected
The local radio station reported that Mr Smith had been guilty of indecency. He has issued a ***writ for slander.*** His local paper repeated the allegation. The editor will be ***sued for slander.***	The local radio station reported that Mr Smith had been guilty of indecency. He has issued a **writ for libel.** His local paper repeated the allegation. The editor will be **sued for libel.**

125 – Licence or License?

Licence is a noun meaning permission, normally with a certificate or document as evidence: "I shall have to renew my **television licence** tomorrow". In a metaphor: "His business is almost **a licence to print money".**

To license, the verb, gives permission to do, to buy or to sell something. Examples: "His restaurant is **licensed to sell alcohol.** To **license** a dog is not necessary. We have **licensed our car** for another year".

Some dictionaries now class **licence** as a verb as well as a noun: **"I shall licence my shop** to sell alcoholic drink". But, in practice, that spelling is rarely accepted in the publishing business. American English uses **license** as both noun and verb.

Licensee is a noun. The person **licensed** is the holder of **a licence** to sell alcohol: "Ivor Jones is **the licensee** of the London Inn". In most countries the possessor of a gun has to be a **licensee.**

NOTE: Licensee spelt with an s seems to be inconsistent with the second c in the noun licence.

Licenser (rarely seen or heard): The granter of a licence.

Unacceptable	Corrected
He has had no ***television license*** since he bought his set five years ago.	He has had no **television licence** since he bought his set five years ago.
Joe had ***no license*** for his car and had no intention of ***licencing it.***	Joe had **no licence** for his car and had no intention of **licensing it.**
The licenser of the inn always visits France once a year to buy his wines.	**The licensee** of the inn always visits France once a year to buy his wines.

Licentious: Unrestrained, immoral, one who takes excessive licence in business or personal conduct. A man was convicted of indecent assault on a young woman and the judge described him as a **revolting, licentious, middle-aged lout.**

Licentiate: One given a licence by a college or governing body to practise a profession, to teach or to preach, confirming competence, sometimes without an academic qualification.

126 – Lighted or Lit?

We take a match and light a fire. **Lighted** or **lit** are the past tenses of the verb **to light.** There is a preference, not a rule.

> The football match was exciting but the floodlights **lit** the pitch so badly at one end that players often missed the ball.
>
> Fire destroyed the haystack when someone walking along the road threw a **lighted** match over the fence.

The preference: **Lit** is the usual past tense and past participle. **Lighted** is preferred as an adjective before a noun, as in **lighted cigarette.** But when the participle is linked to an adverb, **badly lit** streets reads better than ***badly lighted*** streets.

Reported	Preferred
The tragedy would have been avoided if there had been ***a lit lamp*** near the pond.	The tragedy would have been avoided if there had been **a lighted lamp** near the pond.
The classroom was so ***badly lighted*** that we found it difficult to read our books.	The classroom was so **badly lit** that we found it difficult to read our books.

127 – Lightning or Lightening?

Mistakes arise not only from misspelling but from misunderstanding. **Lightning** is an electric flash that precedes thunder. As an adjective, it describes a very quick action.

Lightening is the present participle of the verb **to lighten,** which means to reduce the weight of a load or to bring light to a dark or dull area.

Wrong	Corrected
The ***flash of lightening*** and the thunder that followed frightened the children.	The **flash of lightning** and the thunder that followed frightened the children.
The doctor's diagnosis and medicinal prescriptions put fear into Michael's mind, far from ***lightning his worry.***	The doctor's diagnosis and medicinal prescriptions put fear into Michael's mind, far from **lightening his worry.**

128 – Like or As?

Forget the fact that **you like someone.** That is the verb **to like** and its meaning is understood by five-year-olds. Discussion here is confined to ***like*** when **as** should be used.

The word has become part of so many colloquialisms that, in speech at any rate, the basic rules of Standard English have been discarded. For instance:

> He is spending money ***like*** there's no tomorrow.

instead of

> He is spending money **as if** there were no tomorrow.

The simple advice for business correspondents and for those whose writing appears in memoranda or in a printed page is: ***like*** is not a substitute for **as.**

The general rule is to write the preposition **like** before a noun when no verb follows:

> The children are following their leader **like** sheep.

That sentence is a simile *(see Similes, page 152).* When a verb follows, use **as:**

> The children are following their leader **as** sheep follow one another through a gate.

Wrong	Corrected
He drives carefully, ***like you do.***	He drives carefully, **as you do.**
It looks like it is going to rain.	**It looks as if** it is going to rain.
George has written to you ***like he said he would.***	George has written to you, **as he said he would.**
They will harvest the hay with horses this year, ***like they used to do.***	They will harvest the hay with horses this year, **as they used to do.**
The play was awful, ***like I expected.***	The play was awful, **as I expected.**
She was a fine organist ***like Mary was.***	She was a fine organist, **like Mary.**

129 – Loan or Lend or Borrow?

Dictionaries define **loan** *(a noun)* as the passing of something to someone temporarily – often money for which interest is paid. The bank manager may grant a local grocer a loan of £8000 at 12% interest. **Loan** is common in the United States as a verb: "I can **loan you my car**". ***Loan*** is sometimes used wrongly for **borrow**, which is to obtain something on loan.

To lend, which also implies the temporary use of something, is preferred here, but **to loan** is gaining favour. It is suggested that **"We loaned him our lawnmower"** has a clearer ring than ***"We lent him our lawnmower".***

Reported	Preferred
I will loan you the book when Tom has read it. He *loaned* it last week. The road map of Spain has been returned with frayed edges. ***I am sorry I loaned it.***	**I will lend you the book** when Tom has read it. He **borrowed** it last week. The road map of Spain has been returned with frayed edges. **I am sorry I lent it.**

130 – Loath or Loth or Loathe?

Loath, and the alternative spelling **loth**, are defined as unwilling and reluctant. **"I am loath to travel** the hundred miles to York in my old car in this weather." Preference is to write **loth**, since it is less likely to be confused with **loathe**, although **loath** is more common.

To loathe is to dislike to the point of hatred.

Wrong	Corrected
I loath the journey from Athens to Istanbul and I am *loathe* to go again by car. Why are you *loathe to play* with Harry tomorrow? *You loath Jenny* and you say you are *loathe to meet her brother* Gerald.	**I loathe the journey** from Athens to Istanbul and I am **loth** to go again by car. Why are you **loth to play** with Harry tomorrow? **You loathe Jenny** and you say you are **loath to meet her brother** Gerald.

131 – Majority of people – right   Majority of food – wrong

Majority relates to numbers and not to volume or bulk. The wrongful use of **amount** has become a common mistake. Examples:

> The **majority** (not *amount*) of people working here want a better canteen. They say that the **amount** (not *majority*) of inferior food served now is not acceptable.

When **majority** is meant, **most** is sometimes preferred, because it reads and sounds better: "**Most** of the pears were small".

Wrong	Corrected
The majority of the money is for charity.	**Most** (or **more than half**) of the money is for charity.
The greatest amount of the prizes went to women.	**The majority** (or **most**) of the prizes went to women.

132 – May or Might?

Although often interchanged, there are differences. When referring to the present or future **may** (1) expresses possibilty, doubt, (2) asks for or gives permission. "They **may** be at home now. I **may** win. You **may** join us, if you wish."

Might reduces possibility, increases doubt and can be a suggestion or rebuke. "I **might** win. You **might** move the rubbish before it ferments."

May have goes on expressing possibility, without knowledge of the result. "Julie **may** have gone home."

Might have can suggest greater uncertainty about the present **("Iris might have come home sooner")**, or a theory about a past possibility that we now know did not happen ("He drank from the wrong bottle – **he might have died")**.

Wrong	Corrected
You were foolish to drive without brakes – you *may have been killed.*	You were foolish to drive without brakes – **you might have been killed.**
If police had not come, *the mugger may have got away.*	If police had not come, **the mugger might have got away.**

133 – Metaphors mixed

A metaphor is a comparison between two things written to imply a resemblance. It adds colour to the picture a writer's words try to paint in the mind of the reader. Example:

> The jury's verdict, "Not guilty", snatched the rope from the hands of the hangman.

Metaphors must be consistent – not mixed as in the examples that follow, all taken from books and newspapers, which had a wheel smiling and a rulebook saturated in water:

> He will remain in charge as long as fortune's ***wheel smiles.***
>
> He ***flooded the rulebook*** with his personal obsessions.
>
> We could see that ***intrigue*** had been ***germinating*** for weeks.
>
> The ***sharp tooth*** of remorse began ***to canker his flowery visions.***
>
> The defendant then ***launched into a tissue of lies.***
>
> The ***rising tide*** of his popularity was soon ***obscured*** by the ***winds*** of misfortune.

134 – More than or Over?

Most editors of good newspapers and magazines define a basic difference – **more than** for specific numbers, and **over** for higher, above and beyond.

It is a preference rather than a rule, and in general usage **over** appears more often, even with numbers. Most would say "Old Jim is **over seventy**", not ***"more than seventy",*** although we are more likely to read: "We paid more than £150 for that table" than "over £150". An example below where **more than** is preferred:

Reported	Preferred
Over two hundred bottles of wine and ***more than a ton*** of beef were stolen from the supermarket. An insurance claim of over £2000 is inevitablc.	**More than two hundred bottles** of wine and **over a ton** of beef were stolen from the supermarket. An insurance claim of over/more than £2000 is inevitable.

135 – Mortgagor (Mortgager) or Mortgagee?

A mortgage deed assigns a property as security to a lender or creditor for payment of a loan or debt – like pledging a clock for money lent by a pawnbroker.

The borrower, a person who has bought a house or a company which has taken out a loan, is **the mortgagor** (sometimes spelt **mortgager**). The lender, usually a building society or bank, is **the mortgagee.**

Wrong	Corrected
I bought the house for £75,000 and took a mortgage for £30,000 from Double-X Building Society. I have fallen a year behind with my monthly ***repayments to the mortgagors*** and they have threatened to exercise their rights against ***defaulting mortgagees*** to obtain possession of my house.	I bought the house for £75,000 and took a mortgage for £30,000 from Double-X Building Society. I have fallen a year behind with my monthly **repayments to the mortgagees** and they have threatened to exercise their rights against **defaulting mortgagors** to obtain possession of my house.

136 – Mr T.J. Brown or T.J. Brown Esq. (Esquire)?

The old forms used in letter writing have gradually disappeared. Few, if any, employees now sign letters to their superiors *"Your obedient servant"* as was once the case.

For some reason, **Esquire** has persisted and become common in half of addresses to men. It was once the appendage only for gentlemen of high social or educational rank – MPs, graduates of universities etc. Tradesmen and others were plain **Mr.**

In the United Kingdom nowadays no preference is given to either **Mr** or **Esquire**; not to be addressed as **Esq.** kindles no umbrage. The most common letter-writing mistake now is an undecipherable signature, no identifying block letters underneath and no indication whether **Mr, Mrs, Miss** or **Ms.**

Wrong	Corrected
Mr R.J. Smither ***Esq.,*** of 40 The Loke, Winch.	**Mr** R. J. Smither or R.J. Smither **Esq.,** of 40 The Loke, Winch.

137 – Negatives: double

Two negatives may produce one positive **(not unusual, not uncommon, not impossible, not unlikely).** Such double negatives can sometimes be justified – **not impossible,** for instance, is a shade weaker than possible. But acceptable rules are breached, mainly in speech, with two negatives that become slang. "***I don't know nothing*** about it" is heard often enough.

Wrong	Corrected
They don't need to tell us ***no more*** of that rubbish.	**They don't need** to tell us **any more** of that rubbish.
He didn't never expect his horse to win the Derby.	**He didn't expect** his horse to win the Derby.
They cannot agree, ***not in no circumstances,*** to the new plan for our factory.	They cannot agree **in any circumstances** to the new plan for our factory.
You will not find Tom there, ***I don't believe.***	I don't believe you will find Tom there.

Three negatives in a sentence are heard frequently, spoken in appalling English to create emphasis:

He doesn't never want to speak to him ***no more.***

I never told nobody nothing.

138 – Never

Dictionaries define **never** as at no time, not ever, referring to a period rather than a single occasion. It is often used a little outside its true meaning **in place of not,** when the writer's purpose is to emphasise the negative: "He will **never** have the sense to insure that gold watch".

Wrong	Corrected
My wife was in Victoria Park this morning but she ***never*** saw you.	My wife was in Victoria Park this morning but she **did not** see you.
He has ***never ever*** said a bad word about his employer.	He has **never** said a bad word about his employer.

139 – None was or None were?

That question has no rigid, definitive answer. **None** was originally **not one,** linked to a singular verb: "You made at least ten excuses but **none is** acceptable". We would not write: "*Not one were* acceptable".

But the word has evolved also to mean **not any,** with a plural verb: "**None in my squad are** good enough for the first team".

Advice: (1) To emphasise **not one,** use a singular verb. (2) If the meaning is **all,** use the plural.

> Thirty-six holiday-makers were in the coach when it crashed and none WAS hurt *(emphasis is on not one, no one).*
>
> You want to buy tomatoes but I believe there ARE none left.

Reported	Preferred
The police do not believe me, but *none* of the three boys *have* ever stolen a car.	The police do not believe me, but **none** of the three boys **has** ever stolen a car.
None of us are good enough to take the part of Hamlet.	**None of us is** good enough to take the part of Hamlet.

140 – Numbers (in figures or spell them?)

Uniformity is the first requirement in style. Numbers up to ten in the text look better when spelt (one, three, ten) and those over ten written in figures (11, 14, 101). When numbers are not precise, spell them to read "nearly two thousand houses" and "that was life a hundred years ago".

It is better to write £10m and 10m than £10,000,000 and 10,000,000. The shorter versions are understood at a glance.

Decimals can be misunderstood if written as .65, especially in percentages when the printing is poor and the full stop is indistinct or lost. For clarity write 0.65 and 0.91%.

In some countries commas are used instead of full stops for decimal points (0,65), and commas are omitted from the divisions in figures. The British 10,000 becomes 10 000 in South Africa.

Times and dates written: At 2pm, at two o'clock, or at 1400 hours on January 19, 1994; January 19th, 1994; 19 January, 1994; 19th/1/94 or 19.1.94. Note: 8.1.94 *(day/month/year)* is British style for 8 January, 1994; 1.8.94 *(month/day/year)* is American.

141 – Only

Only is solely, at no other time, in no other place, for no other reason: "I work overtime **only on Thursdays".** In speech, we hear "I ***only work overtime*** on Thursdays". That is ambiguous. ***"I only speak*** to Tom" is not the same as "I speak **only to Tom".**

Mistakes in meaning are rare, but **only** is seldom placed as near as possible to the word or phrase to which it refers – slovenly English, seen and heard everywhere, every day. The meaning may not be misunderstood, but a change of sense can result, as the words of this estate agent suggest:

We advertise only properties for sale in the Gazette.

(Only properties for sale advertised – not those to let.)

We advertise properties for sale only in the Gazette.

(We do not advertise in the Chronicle or other papers.)

Careless	Correct
(1) ***George only paid me today*** for the two sheep he bought more than a year ago.	**George paid me only today** for the two sheep he bought more than a year ago.
(2) His flight was diverted to Japan and Taiwan but ***he only reached Australia one day late.***	His flight was diverted to Japan and Taiwan but **he reached Australia only one day late.**
(3) The workers at our factory ***only walked out when*** their wage claim was rejected.	The workers at our factory **walked out only when** their wage claim was rejected.

NOTE: **Only** refers to **today** in the first corrected example (1), to **one day late** in (2) and to **when the wage claim was rejected** in (3). In all the above, only is an adverb.

Only is also written as an adjective: "George Sampson was **the only man** to speak; and it was the only reason he came".

Only as a conjunction is used mainly to take the place of **but. "**It is a pity you have to go so soon, **only** I know you have to be home by six o'clock." The conjunction ***only,*** however, does not contribute to an elegant phrase.

142 – On to or Onto?

Not all dictionaries list ***onto.*** In an old one it is described as colloquial and vulgar. But it is now commonly used. The purist still advises us to avoid ***onto*** as one word, although, having written "**into** the room", it is difficult to disallow such examples as these:

He jumped onto the horse. I stuck a label onto the bag.

That makes sense and is comparable to "He jumped into the river". But ***to*** seems to be superfluous in the two ***onto*** examples: "He jumped on the horse" and "I stuck a label on the bag". **On** and **to** are usually distinctly separate and will in no case be wrong: "He passed the ball **on to** the next man".

Reported	Correct
Fog came down suddenly at Amsterdam and our aircraft flew ***onto*** London Heathrow to land in sunshine.	Fog came down suddenly at Amsterdam and our aircraft flew **on to** London Heathrow to land in sunshine.

143 – Didn't ought to – wrong Shouldn't ought to – wrong

Ought becomes part of many ugly phrases, mainly in speech. It is a little more emphatic than **should;** it insists on a duty or adherence to a principle. Do not use ***ought*** with ***didn't*** and ***shouldn't.***

Wrong	Corrected
We didn't ought to move into the new offices until after the summer holiday.	**We ought not** to move into the new offices until after the summer holiday.
I shouldn't ought to pay as much for a holiday near home.	**I ought not** to pay as much for a holiday near home.

Should and **should not** are alternatives to **ought** and **ought not.** In speech especially, **ought** and **ought not** have a little more impact. For instance:

You **ought not** to risk swimming in that treacherous sea.

is a more persuasive warning than "You **should not** risk swimming in that treacherous sea".

144 – Passed or Past?

Passed is the past tense of the verb **to pass.** It has a number of meanings. "His car **passed** (went by) me. His daughter **has passed** (taken successfully) her examination. The council **passed** (approved) plans for a new town hall."

Past refers to a former time. "He is a **past** *(adjective)* **chairman.**" "He earned a lot of money **in the past** *(noun).*" **"It's past** its sell-by date *(preposition).*" **"We walked past** *(adverb).*"

Wrong	Corrected
Tom past his driving test and it was *passed midnight* when he came home.	**Tom passed his driving test** and it was **past midnight** when he came home.
At 72, John is well *passed the age* to be running in the London marathon.	At 72, John is well **past the age** to be running in the London marathon.

145 – Persecute or Prosecute?

Both words imply action against a person or persons. **Persecute** (to suppress, to oppress, to harass) is sometimes wrongly written for **prosecute** (to accuse in a court of law).

Persecution usually has religious, psychological or racial reasons. **Prosecute** also has a non-legal, crude meaning for some, telling of action to achieve or to follow up something: "He **prosecuted** with enthusiasm the target to raise £50,000".

Wrong	Corrected
The persecution of so many for shoplifting compelled *the persecutor* to postpone his holiday.	**The prosecution** of so many for shoplifting compelled **the prosecutor** to postpone his holiday.
To prosecute them by boycotting their shops was wicked but not illegal.	**To persecute** them by boycotting their shops was wicked but not illegal.
The police will not charge the old man, so *I shall persecute him* myself.	The police will not charge the old man, so **I shall prosecute** him myself.

146 – Personal or Personnel?

Personal is the adjective of the noun **person** (a human being). A **personal opinion** is strictly a private opinion.

Personally, an adverb, means in person: "Your new car is expected tomorrow and I shall deliver it to you **personally**". It is too often written as a superfluous word, usually for emphasis: "***I personally believe*** that the price is too high".

Personable describes someone as of good appearance and attitude. **Personality** places distinctive characteristics on a person: "She is **a weak personality** who falls victim to the plausible salesman". **Personalty** is personal property.

Personnel is a group of people who may be staff in a business or serving with the military. Many companies have **personnel managers** or directors to deal with all staff matters.

Wrong	Corrected
It is ***a personnel matter*** for the chairman to select any employee for redundancy.	It is **a personal matter** for the chairman to select any employee for redundancy.
Superfluous word	**Preferred**
You can sack Tim Mudd, but I *personally* think you have a moral duty not to do so.	You can sack Tim Mudd, but I think you have a moral duty not to do so.

147 – Piece or Peace?

Piece and **peace** are among the most elementary errors, through misspelling rather than misunderstanding. Even the uneducated know that **piece** is a part of anything (a bit) when spoken, and that **peace** means freedom from hostility and tranquility.

Wrong	Corrected
My mind was at piece with the world as I sat alone in the church. Suddenly a stone crashed through a window and ***a peace of glass*** struck me.	**My mind was at peace** with the world as I sat alone in the church. Suddenly a stone crashed through a window and **a piece of glass** struck me.

148 – The Plurals of Nouns

Mistakes sometimes occur when the plural of a noun is formed. They are spelling errors but the reason is usually the writer's failure to remember or to understand one of the several changes that are possible *(See Nouns in Parts of Speech).*

Leading the doubts are **tomatoes** and **potatoes** – often written wrongly as ***tomatos*** and ***potatos.*** And ***ladys*** instead of **ladies** is familiar, occasionally in advertisements. ***Lady's,*** with the apostrophe, used as the plural of **lady,** has also been seen many times in print.

Wrong	Corrected
The ***ladys'*** section of our society meets on Wednesdays in the town hall.	The **ladies'** section of our society meets on Wednesdays in the town hall.
Mrs Plumm said the ***Plummes*** would be going to Guernsey in September.	Mrs Plumm said the **Plumms** would be going to Guernsey in September.
It will be two ***weekes*** before we know the result.	It will be two **weeks** before we know the result.
We spent the whole day in the garden harvesting ***potatos*** and ***tomatos*** but we heard no ***cuckooes.***	We spent the whole day in the garden harvesting **potatoes** and **tomatoes** but we heard no **cuckoos.**
Your ***radios*** tone is better than any I have heard on any ***radioes*** in our shop.	Your **radio's** tone is better than any I have heard on any **radios** in our shop.
The storm did much damage to ***rooves*** of twenty houses.	The storm did much damage to **roofs** of twenty houses.
Lock your doors securely at night – there are many ***thiefs*** about.	Lock your doors securely at night – there are many **thieves** about.
The ***mouses*** in our garden shed have eaten some of the ***potatos*** I dug last week.	The **mice** in our garden shed have eaten some of the **potatoes** I dug last week.
Farmer Brown has decided to reduce the number of ***sheeps*** he rears and to concentrate on ***deers*** in his woodland.	Farmer Brown has decided to reduce the number of **sheep** he rears and to concentrate on **deer** in his woodland.

149 – Plural nouns and Singular verbs Mixed

The plural of a verb *(are, were, have)* is often wrongly written when the singular **(is, was, has)** is required. A plural noun **(men)** is followed by a plural verb **(were)**, as the singular noun **(man)** takes the singular verb **(was)**. Mistakes are common.

Wrong	Corrected
The cost of the new houses *were* out of our reach.	**The cost** of the new houses **was** out of our reach.
There has been cases of men working 18 hours a day to satisfy demand for the shoes.	**There have been cases** of men working 18 hours a day to satisfy demand for the shoes.
Each of the seven runners in the race *were* at fault.	**Each** of the seven runners in the race **was** at fault.
The poor quality of the farmer's potatoes *make* the problem of selling them more difficult than in any year since 1987.	**The poor quality** of the farmer's potatoes **makes** the problem of selling them more difficult than in any year since 1987.
Land bought from the Aggin and Hill estates, including 70 hectares of woodland, *are* to be sold again.	**Land bought** from the Aggin and Hill estates, including 70 hectares of woodland, **is** to be sold again.

150 – Plurals of Compound Nouns

No firm rule decides the correct plural of a compound noun. The general practice is to apply the plural sign to the more or most important part in the compound: **Governors**-general, **passers**-by, **runners**-up, lieutenant-**generals.** But both parts carry the plural in **men-servants.** In compounds without a hyphen, we normally write **handfuls, handouts** and **bucketfuls.**

Wrong	Corrected
We have *three son-in-laws* and *two daughter-in-laws.*	We have **three sons-in-law** and **two daughters-in-law.**
The *lieutenants-colonel* hope to be *commander-in-chiefs.*	The **lieutenant-colonels** hope to be **commanders-in-chief.**

151 – Plutocracy or Autocracy?

A plutocrat and **an autocrat** can be the same person. The difference is money. In **a plutocracy** all power is with the wealthy. In **an autocracy** uncrontrolled power is in one person, often a despot who did not acquire absolute authority through wealth but through revolution or insurrection.

Both are dictatorships in the manner of Adolf Hitler's **autocratic rule** of Germany, 1934-45. But **autocrat** and **plutocrat** are words occasionally fastened critically to an employer or controller of a voluntary organisation.

Wrong	Corrected
A plutocracy in the African republic was at the absolute command of one man – a colonel who had come out of prison, with a gun but no money.	**An autocracy** in the African republic was at the absolute command of one man – a colonel who had come out of prison, with a gun but no money.

152 – Poor or Pour or Pore?

Howlers abound, with failure to spell correctly attributed to misunderstanding of meanings. All three words have entirely different definitions.

Poor has a wide meaning – short of money, needy, barren, not good, feeble, of inferior quality, inadequate and sometimes used to imply sympathy: **"The poor man** has lost his job".

To pore over a document is to study it intently. **A pore** is a minute opening in the skin through which perspiration passes. **Pores** are also found in materials such as bricks.

To pour is to cause a liquid to flow, perhaps to empty a jug. A crowd is sometimes said ***to pour from a stadium,*** but that offends some of us as a mixed metaphor.

Wrong	Corrected
I pored the tea accidentally on the book *the pour girl poored over,* as she sat in the armchair studying hard for next week's examination.	**I poured the tea** accidentally on the book **the poor girl pored over,** as she sat in the armchair studying hard for next week's examination.

153 – Practical or Practicable?

Practical means that experience or special knowledge is used when a job or commitment is undertaken. Examples:

Tom Trevethick is a first-class **practical** plumber.

Arthur has **practical** experience of making wine.

Practicable means workable, achievable, feasible, something that can be done, at least in theory. It could refer to the menu for a dinner party or the plan for a house. Examples:

It is not **practicable** to grow fruit on such dry soil.

The river is in flood and it is not **practicable** to cross.

Wrong	Corrected
Sam hasn't a *practicable approach* to the job of putting up a garden shed.	Sam hasn't a **practical approach** to the job of putting up a garden shed.
If it is practical, we shall be glad to build your garage on that plot.	**If it is practicable,** we shall be glad to build your garage on that plot.

154 – Practically

Practically has acquired a meaning that often contradicts its original definition: in practice, in effect, in a practical manner. Some dictionaries still offer that interpretation with no alternative. But **practically** is now generally spoken and written as **nearly and almost.** "He left yesterday and **will be practically there.**"

Reported	Meaning
Tom was *practically beaten* but they had two more games to play.	Tom was on the verge of defeat. OR It wasn't yet certain. Tom could still win.
I practically bought the farm last night.	I almost bought the farm last night but didn't. OR The farm is now almost mine.

155 – Practice or Practise?

Practice is a noun. Examples: "**A doctor's practice. It's the practice** to sow the seeds in April. **One practice** on the piano each day should be enough".

Practise is a verb. Examples: "**She practised** the piano each day. You should **practise tennis** with your brother".

Wrong	Corrected
The practise here is for women to have first choice of tennis court.	**The practice** here is for women to have first choice of tennis court.
They practiced hard all season at snooker but no one won a cup or medal.	**They practised** hard all season at snooker but no one won a cup or medal.
Practise for juniors will be on four evenings a week. Players are also encouraged *to practice* at home.	**Practice** for juniors will be on four evenings a week. Players are also encouraged **to practise** at home.

156 – Prefix and Suffix?

Prefix: A syllable or letters that, when placed in front of a word, with or without a hyphen, changes the meaning. **Un-** is widely used to create negatives – unexplained, unfit, unload. Other examples:

anti- (against) *anticlimax*	**arch-** (chief, first) *archbishop*	**hyper-** (above normal) *hypermarket*
fore- (before) *foretell*	**pre-** and **ante-** (before) *prearrange antenatal*	**semi-** (half) *semi-colon*
contra- (against) *contradiction*	**inter-** (between) *intermarry*	**bi-** (two, twice) *bilingual*

Mistakes do occur with **anti-** and **ante-**: *anteseptic* (wrong) for **antiseptic,** *anti-room* (wrong) for **ante-room.**

Suffix: A syllable or letters added at the end of words to extend or qualify meaning. Example: **-less** indicates "without", as in senseless, careless, boneless, aimless, painless.

-ish (similar) *snobbish*	**-monger** (dealer) *fishmonger*	**-stead** (place) *homestead*

157 – Presume or Assume?

To assume (1) is to take upon oneself, to take for granted (e.g., "**Tom assumes all powers** to himself on the factory floor"), and (2) to accept what has been written as the truth, but without proof (e.g., "**Let's assume** for the moment that George is capable of designing the house").

To presume (1) is to accept a statement as accurate, to infer (e.g., "**I presume you will,** as two years ago, rejoin us on returning from Egypt?") and (2) has a sense of dare, to carry on without previous permission (e.g., "**I presumed to question** the judge at my trial").

Either is sometimes correct. "**I assumed/presumed** (took for granted) that you would accept responsibility for the mistake."

The nouns are **assumption** and **presumption.**

Reported	Preferred/Correct
Bob presumes his place in the House of Lords on the death of his brother.	**Bob assumes his place** in the House of Lords on the death of his brother.
Dr Livingstone, *I assume.*	Dr Livingstone, **I presume.**
On *the presumption* that Mark has paid for last month's delivery, another load of potatoes will be sent.	On **the assumption** that Mark has paid for last month's delivery, another load of potatoes will be sent.

158 – Prey or Pray?

An animal preys upon another and kills it for food. **To prey,** therefore, is to seize by violence, to spoil and to plunder. Outside animal life, a person may fall victim to an enemy in business. The victim is **the prey.**

To pray is to entreat, to beseech, to petition and, in basic sense, to offer prayer to the Almighty.

Wrong	Corrected
We prey that no harm will come to our son Patrick in Lapland this winter.	**We pray** that no harm will come to our son Patrick in Lapland this winter.

159 – Principal or Principle?

Mistakes are astonishing. An English college advertised in headline type for a ***Principle lecturer*** in law with possible election to a professorship and for a ***Principle lecturer*** in organic chemistry. If the polytechnic issued it, the newspaper's advertisement department failed to correct it.

Principal *(noun):* Head of something (e.g., the **principal** of a college), the chief, a leader. A sum of money lent to produce interest is **the principal.** As an adjective, it means first in importance, leading, main (e.g., **the principal speaker).**

Principle *(noun):* An ideal (e.g., absolute honesty), theory (e.g., the way a person aims to conduct his life), basic rule of morality (e.g., no deceit, no dishonesty, clean living). The word is sometimes adapted as an adjective: "Our **principled aims** are to protect the company's integrity".

The examples below are among many taken from publications of repute in their geographical or subject areas:

Wrong	Corrected
Strict ***religious principals*** required the family to observe the fast from dawn until dusk.	Strict **religious principles** required the family to observe the fast from dawn until dusk.
Wanted: Principle tenor for the City Choir.	**Wanted: Principal tenor** for the City Choir.
The principal in all games at our school is fair play.	**The principle in all games** at our school is fair play.
London is becoming one of the three ****principle centres*** in the world securities market. **In a bold newspaper headline.*	London is becoming one of the three **principal centres** in the world securities' market.
The principle objectives are to maintain interest in nursing and to encourage nurses who might be considering returning to work.	**The principal objectives** are to maintain interest in nursing and to encourage nurses who might be considering returning to work.
Having ***agreed in principal,*** what should we do now?	Having **agreed in principle,** what should we do now?

160 – Prohibit or Inhibit?

To prohibit is to forbid, to prevent. "The airline has decided **to prohibit** smoking on all flights from January 1st. It is **a prohibition** that will lose them many passengers but will probably attract many new ones."

To inhibit is to hinder, to hold back, to restrain. "The effect of the accident in which 37 people were killed was **to inhibit** Tom from wanting to drive a train again. He has **an inhibition** that is likely to be with him like a nightmare for the rest of his life."

Wrong	Corrected
He is inhibited from entering the club after the affray last week and the committee's decision has *left him prohibited* about applying to join elsewhere.	**He is prohibited** from entering the club after the affray last week and the committee's decision has **left him inhibited** about applying to join elsewhere.
The strict parking controls applied by traffic wardens in South Winch *prohibit me* from shopping there.	The strict parking controls applied by traffic wardens in South Winch **inhibit me** from shopping there.

161 – Prophecy or Prophesy?

The chance of confusion or misunderstanding is small, even if **prophecy** is written wrongly instead of **prophesy,** or the other way round. But **a prophecy** is a noun and **to prophesy** is a verb. They foretell the future. In speech they are readily identifiable; prophecy ends **-see,** prophesy ends **-si.**

Wrong	Corrected
The prophesy of the local crystal-gazer scared us and we said *we would prophecy* trouble for his family if he repeated the nonsense.	**The prophecy** of the local crystal-gazer scared us and we said **we would prophesy** trouble for his family if he repeated the nonsense.
To prophecy peace for a hundred years is *a prophesy* too good to believe.	**To prophesy** peace for a hundred years is **a prophecy** too good to believe.

162 – Proscribe or Prescribe?

To proscribe is to denounce with authority, to prohibit, to reject. A government may **proscribe an insecticide** such as DDT, which has been banned in several countries.

To prescribe is to set or lay down laws or rules that direct action or control. **Doctors prescribe remedies** for illness and injury. Both words are sometimes wrongly written because of their similar spelling and pronunciation.

Wrong	Corrected
A television programme was *prescribed for children* because of its violent content, but *proscribed for adults* because of warnings it carried about the dangers in unlit roads in darkness.	A television programme was **proscribed for children** because of its violent content, but **prescribed for adults** because of warnings it carried about the dangers in unlit roads in darkness.

163 – Pupil or Student or Undergraduate or Graduate or Post-graduate?

A boy or girl who attends a school from the age of four or five is referred to as **a pupil.** The word is also used for a person of any age who is taking instruction privately from a scholar.

A student is engaged in a course of study at a further education college or institute, or university, from the age of 16 upwards. Pupils are sometimes called *students,* leaving the wrong impression of ages.

An undergraduate is a student at a college or university who aims to take an academic degree, to become **a graduate** after two, three or four years. He or she may then enrol at a university as **a post-graduate** to pursue studies, often with a high element of research.

Reported	Corrected
Little Jenefer has become a *student* at St Mary's Primary School. She will be six next month.	Little Jenefer has become a **pupil** at St Mary's Primary School. She will be six next month.

164 – Quite

Quite (1) denotes completely, surprisingly, entirely, without limitations: "He has worked **quite skilfully.** The result is a **quite beautiful** piece of pottery". That is the word's basic meaning with extreme words – **quite** disgusting, **quite** extra-ordinary, **quite** exceptional, **quite** unacceptable.

But (2) **quite** has evolved also to imply moderately, almost, and fairly with moderate words – **quite pleasant** – and even to be sarcastically critical with faint praise. "We went to our neighbours' house for dinner and had **quite a pleasant evening.** Our boys enjoyed it, even if their calls for second helpings were **not quite the way to behave** in a neighbour's house!"

Quite is more appropriately spoken than written – the voice intones meaning and emphasis. It is ambiguous as used below because, in text without a voice, it could have been a sarcastic comment on Ben's payment.

Ambiguous	Intended meaning
It was *quite generous* of Ben to pay for our lunch at the pub. We *quite enjoyed* it.	It was **very generous** of Ben to pay for our lunch at the pub. We **much enjoyed** it.

The most colloquial use of **quite** is probably as an affirmative – "Yes" or "I agree". Example:

Mr Thomas: He is out of mind to want to climb that cliff,

Mr Richard: "Quite!"

Learning by Example

COMMON MISTAKES

Part five – R to W

165 – Replace or Displace?

To displace something is to take it from its accustomed or proper place. A machine in a factory may be **displaced** because it has become useless and taken to the scrap heap or to the premises of a buyer. New equipment, of course, can fill the space; that would be **a replacement.**

To replace is a positive act of putting something back in its original place, or to provide a substitute. A book, having been read, may be **replaced** (placed again) on the bookshelf; or **replaced** by one with another title.

Wrong	Corrected
A bomb dropped from a military aircraft into the desert. A massive quantity of sand was *replaced.*	A bomb dropped from a military aircraft into the desert. A massive quantity of sand was **displaced.**
I *displaced* my old Raleigh cycle with a new one.	I **replaced** my old Raleigh cycle with a new one.

166 – The Reason/Why/Because

All three words often appear in one sentence when one would be sufficient. There are few better examples of superfluous language – **tautology* – when they are interlocked.

Because is emphatic about the cause of something – on account of, since. A woman fell **because** of ice on the pavement.

Reason shows motive, cause, explanation, excuse and expresses the logical, factual answer to a question.

Why expresses cause, purpose or reason.

Reported	Correct
The reason why you are so short of money ***is because*** you spend so much of your wages on beer.	**The reason** you are so short of money is that you spend so much of your wages on beer.
The manager said that ***the reason*** you were not promoted ***was because*** you are late for work too often.	The manager said you were not promoted **because** you are late for work too often.
Why Bill was driving fast when the police stopped him ***was because*** he was late for an important appointment.	Bill was driving fast **because** he was late for an important appointment when the police stopped him.
The reason he could not pay the bill ***was on account of*** losing his cheque book.	He could not pay the bill **because** he had lost his cheque book.

***Tautology:** The same word or idea unnecessarily repeated:

Grateful thanks. No *other* alternative. Revert *back.*

Outside *of.* Follow *after.* Rise *up.* Repeat *again.*

Tautology	Corrected
Join together the broken pieces and ***give*** the old chair to Edith as a ***free gift.*** She knows its ***original source*** and its ***past history.***	**Join** the broken pieces and **give** the old chair to Edith. She knows **its origin** and **its history.**

167 – Reporting the words of others

Letters, reports, memoranda and essays often quote the words of politicians, authors, business people and friends. They are written as:

Speech reported (1) DIRECT: The exact words of a speaker, reported in the first person within quotation marks. Example:

> Mr Brown said: "I have decided to postpone my retirement for at least another year, and I expect to see the company's cash problems solved in my time here. ***Neither*** the factory workers ***or*** the office staff will have any need to worry about their jobs at this point in time".

OR

Speech reported (2) INDIRECT: The speaker's words reported in the third person, without quotation marks, usually produce an edited, compact version, correcting any grammatical slips (**nor,** not ***or***) and eliminating slovenly language:

> Mr Brown said that he had decided to postpone his retirement for at least another year and he expected the company's cash problems to be solved in that time. **Neither** the factory workers **nor** the office staff needed to worry about their jobs for the time being.

That conversion shows the indirect reporting in harmony with the reporting verb (**said**), which is normally in the past tense:

> He said **that**... He reported **that**... He claimed **that**...

with following verb tenses in sequence:

> He said **that he wanted** ***(not wants)*** to visit Australia.

An alternative, retaining the present tense without directly quoting a statement, is sometimes used:

> **Mr Brown says** he will postpone his retirement for at least another year and **he expects** the company's cash problems to be solved in that time.

Wrong	Corrected
Mr Downing said he ***does not*** believe our troops ***will*** be at greater risk than they ***had been*** in the past week.	Mr Downing said he **did not** believe our troops **would** be at greater risk than they **had been** in the past week.

168 – Respective/Respectively The former/The latter First-mentioned/Last-mentioned

On rare occasions one of the pairs is needed, but advice here is to avoid them if possible. They often compel a reader to begin a sentence again to identify a name or object, as seen in the first colum of the first example below. Sometimes there is confusion over which word is referred to as **first-mentioned** or **the latter.** For clarity, repeat the word or words.

Reported	Preferred
Pensioners, who will receive money as well as a Christmas gift, and the company's workers, should report to the chairman's office at 10am and 11am ***respectively.***	Pensioners, who will receive money as well as a Christmas gift, should report to the chairman's office at 10am, and the company's workers should report at 11am.
Ushers at the murder trial that begins today must see that police witnesses and the public use the ***respective*** front and side entrances.	Ushers at the murder trial that begins today must see that police witnesses use the front entrance and the public the side entrance.
Problems have arisen for Albert, youngest of the four brothers, Tom, George and Harold in finding employment, but the ***first-mentioned*** has an interview tomorrow and the ***last-mentioned*** has one next week.	Problems have arisen for Albert, Tom, George and Harold in finding employment, but Albert, youngest of the four brothers, has an interview tomorrow and Harold has one next week
Lazenby and Co. are certain to win the Emden award for exports, with Smith and Co. taking the Plast certificate in second place, but ***the latter*** will be unlucky not to beat ***the former***.	Lazenby and Co. are certain to win the Emden award for exports but will be lucky to beat Smith and Co., who, in second place, will take the Plast certificate.
There was a time when Ivor Jones always came top of the poll in local elections, but Ike Jacobs beat him this year, so ***the former*** lost his seat for the first time.	There was a time when Ivor Jones always came top of the poll in local elections, but he lost his seat this year for the first time, beaten by Ike Jacobs.

169 – Responsible

Only people take or bear **responsibility;** things do not. A **responsible person** is one who is answerable, legally or morally, for the discharge of a duty, and is able to distinguish between right and wrong.

Wrong	Corrected
The hurricane was *responsible* for the destruction of ten thousand fir trees.	The hurricane **caused** the destruction of ten thousand fir trees.

170 – Rise or Raise?

To raise a car to inspect it underneath is to hoist it on a ramp. **To raise** a loan from the bank is to obtain money.

A car will **rise** on a ramp. Wages and temperatures **rise.** Anything **rising** is moving upwards. **We cannot rise something.**

Wrong	Corrected
He was quick *to rise the cash,* and we should *raise from our seats* to cheer.	He was quick **to raise the cash,** and we should **rise from our seats** to cheer.

171 – Rouse or Arouse?

The simple definition for both words is to awaken. But **arouse** is generally accepted as awakening a person's feelings, perhaps with doubt, fear or curiosity.

Rouse takes us into action. A soldier may be **roused** from his sleep to take up guard duties. A footballer's vicious tackle may **rouse** an opponent to strike him.

Reported	Preferred
Tim's absence *rouses* doubts about his promise to pay money he owes us.	Tim's absence **arouses** doubts about his promise to pay the the money he owes us.

172 – Sentences misconstructed

When a word or phrase is wrongly placed, a sentence can become unbalanced, loose or absurd, even if the meaning is obvious. Examples (including one which has a town hall walking along the river bank):

Misconstructed	Intended meaning
Walking across the street ***my glasses*** fell off.	**As I was walking** across the street, my glasses fell off.
The old ***town hall can be seen walking*** along the river bank.	The old town hall can be seen **as you walk** along the river bank.
Did you see the ***mountains crossing the bridge?***	Did you see the mountains **as you crossed** the bridge?
They nearly saw two cars collide at the crossroads.	They saw two cars **nearly collide** at the crossroads.
All the cars they sold at yesterday's auction ***are not*** completely worn out.	**Not all the cars** they sold at yesterday's auction are completely worn out.
It is difficult ***to really find a true friend*** in a foreign country when you do not speak the language.	It is difficult **to find a really true friend** in a foreign country when you do not speak the language.
Your father has won the top award at this year's horticultural show and he is ***in a great state of excitement.***	Your father has won the top award at this year's horticultural show and he is in **a state of great excitement.**
They ***not only scorched*** the kitchen walls but the ceiling when their frying pan caught alight.	They **scorched not only** the kitchen walls but also the ceiling when their frying pan caught alight.
They ***not only searched*** the wood but also the adjoining common.	They **searched not only** the wood but also the adjoining common.
Tom squandered every pound of the hundreds given to him by ***his girl-friend in a drunken orgy.***	**Tom, in a drunken orgy,** squandered every pound of the hundreds given to him by his girl-friend.

173 – Sewer or Sewage or Sewerage?

The word **sewer** causes problems for the few who write memoranda or reports on the subject. It is a drain, usually a pipeline underground, although there are open sewers cut into the surface.

Sewage is the excrement and other matter discharged through the sewers. A city council reported: **"Sewage disposal** is a problem in the old part of our city".

Sewerage is the system of pipes and channels through which the sewage passes. Every year many villages in the United Kingdom are connected for the first time to modern sewerage.

Wrong	Corrected
Many South African township homes ***still need sewage;*** the cost will run into millions of Rands. ***Sewerage disposal*** is not satisfactory because of the increase in population. The sewers are too small.	Many South African township homes **still need sewerage;** the cost will run into millions of Rands. **Sewage disposal** is not satisfactory because of the increase in population. The sewers are too small.

174 – Sew or Sow?

Mistakes often appear when **sew** and **sow** are written – not when spoken, as pronunciation is the same. **To sew** is to stitch together with needle and thread. **To sow** is to scatter or to plant seed on ground. The simple breakdown of tenses, which may trip some, is:

> I **sew** (I sewed, I have sewn) new cuffs to my husband's shirts.
>
> I **sow** (I sowed, I have sown) turnip seed in my vegetable plot.

Wrong	Corrected
When I have sown up your coat pocket, we can go into the garden ***to sew the bean seeds*** which should have been ***sewn*** ten days ago.	**When I have sewn up** your coat pocket, we can go into the garden **to sow the bean seeds** which should have been **sown** ten days ago.

175 – Sight or Site or Cite?

The three words have identical pronunciation. In speech, there are few problems, but transcribing them after dictation requires a clear understanding of their meanings.

Sight, being the ability to see or something seen, is easy. The sunrise on the Indian Ocean is a **beautiful sight** from the seafront in Durban. **A gun has a sight** through which to aim.

A site is a place where something happens or has happened. More than two hundred men work on a large site where houses are being built. But a **site** can be any place — the area of an ancient battle, for instance.

Cite is to mention, to summon, to quote, to name. **A woman cited** another woman in a divorce action. **A lawyer cited** a judge's interpretation of property law to support his plea.

Wrong	Corrected
We sited the builder's promise to the council to keep ***the sight*** tidy. It was to be a pleasant ***cite*** for critical eyes.	**We cited** the builder's promise to the council to keep **the site** tidy. It was to be a pleasant **sight** for critical eyes.

176 – Similes (overworked)

A Simile is a direct comparison between two things or two acts that are different — written to describe one of them vividly, dramatically or more clearly. **Like** or **as** usually introduces the comparison. Examples:

> Watching dubbed films is like washing your feet with your socks on *(Daily Telegraph).*

> Swift as a shadow, short as any dream, brief as the lightning in the collied night *(Shakespeare).*

Fresh and striking comparisons are the marks of a creative and imaginative writer. To be effective, a simile should not be worn-out clichés such as:

Drunk as a lord. Cool as a cucumber. Like a bull at a gate.

Hot as hell. Quiet as a mouse. Like as two peas.

Like water off a duck's back. Different as chalk from cheese.

177 – Special or Especial?

Special is a much used word meaning distinctive, particular, not ordinary, original. **A special vegetarian meal** may be cooked for a distinguished visitor.

Especial, which is not so common, has a similar meaning but also embellishes the word or words it describes with a sense of exceptional or superior.

> **An especial welcome** awaited the party when they returned from the Far East. Two thousand were there.

As the difference in the two adjectives is a fine one, they are often interchangeable. The same cannot be said when **-ly** is added to form the adverbs **specially** and **especially.** The meaning then almost always varies or is transformed, although one can sometimes replace the other.

Specially points to something that is said or done for a particular reason, aim or purpose. The puddings were made **specially** (expressly, deliberately) for Christmas.

Especially means exceptionally, excessively, mainly, above all, particularly. "In our family, **father especially,** prefers to spend his holidays in Devon or Cornwall."

Reported	Correct/preferred
The route we take in the coach from Rome to London cannot be changed ***especially*** for the convenience of your Mr Robinson and his wife.	The route we take in the coach from Rome to London cannot be changed **specially** for the convenience of your Mr Robinson and his wife.
We like to visit two or three game reserves when we are in South Africa, ***specially*** the Kruger National Park.	We like to visit two or three game reserves when we are in South Africa, **especially** the Kruger National Park.
Your ***especial*** ability to thatch the roofs of those cottages will make you a good living.	Your **special** ability to thatch the roofs of those cottages will make you a good living.
Young people ***specially*** should not start smoking, as many of them do even before they leave school.	Young people **especially** should not start smoking, as many of them do even before they leave school.

The roses were bought **especially** (or **specially**) for her.

178 – Spouse

Spouse is a word now confined mainly to legal documents and religious orders. It means a partner in marriage, husband or wife. It is sometimes misunderstood as reference only to the wife. An example of its rare use:

> All Winch City Council members and **their spouses** attended the Mayor's and Mayoress's 50th wedding anniversary celebrations.

179 – Stationery or Stationary?

Fifty students with university entrance qualifications were questioned on the meanings. Almost half wrote the wrong answer and most confessed afterwards that they had guessed.

Stationery: Writing paper, envelopes and similar materials found in a stationer's shop and general stores. Link the word envelope, with its three **e's**, with stationEry in the memory as a clue to the correct spelling.

Stationary: Stopped, standing still, not moving. Usually refers to vehicles that are stationary.

Wrong	Corrected
That ***stationery van*** outside the newsagent's shop is delivering a ***big load of stationary*** and books.	That **stationary van** outside the newsagent's shop is delivering a **big load of stationery** and books.

180 – Statue or Statute?

A statue is an image carved or moulded out of stone, metal, wood or pliable substance. **A statute** is a law, an Act of Parliament to be placed on the statute book.

Wrong	Corrected
Nelson's Column, with its 17ft ***statute*** of the admiral, attracts thousands to Trafalgar Square every day. Nearby, ***statues*** are enacted in the Houses of Parliament.	Nelson's Column, with its 17ft **statue** of the admiral, attracts thousands to Trafalgar Square every day. Nearby, **statutes** are enacted in the Houses of Parliament.

181 – Straight or Strait?

The adjective or adverb **straight** and the verb **straighten** should present little difficulty. "The 100-metre track has a slight curve in it; **we went straight to the committee** to complain and **they decided to straighten it** to ensure **a straight line** between starting post and finish. The chairman is **a straight man** – upright in character."

Strait is narrow. The Strait of Dover (narrow). **Strait**-laced (strict). **Strait**-jacket (closely confined). **Straitened** = to restrict, to limit: **straitened** circumstances (poverty).

Wrong	Corrected
He lives ***in straightened circumstances*** since he lost his job on the farm.	He lives **in straitened circumstances** since he lost his job on the farm.
She is in dire straights after an illness, but she is doing her best to ***straiten her financial affairs.***	**She is in dire straits** after an illness, but she is doing her best to **straighten her financial affairs.**

182 – Subsequent or Consequent?

Subsequent means following in time, place or order. **Subsequent** to a violent demonstration, the police introduced new regulations to protect local inhabitants. **Subsequently,** a television series on the subject was made.

A consequent act or occurrence is a natural or necessary development as a result of a particular deed or event. If a boys' school decides to admit girls, **the consequent increase** in numbers will mean the employment of extra staff.

Reported	Intended meaning
Japhta fell and broke his leg. ***Subsequently,*** he was unable to take up the new job he had obtained.	Japhta fell and broke his leg. **Consequently,** he was unable to take up the new job he had obtained.
Ruth failed her final nursing examination last year, but she passed at ***the consequent attempt.***	Ruth failed her final nursing examination last year, but she passed at **the subsequent attempt.**

183 – Suppress or Repress?

Dictionary definitions are almost the same. Restraint is common to both. The difference is the degree of restraint. **Suppress** is stronger than **repress.**

To suppress is to put down, to overpower, to conceal. **A disturbance** in a restaurant **may be suppressed** when hooligans are arrested. Governments have been known to **suppress news.**

To repress is to hold back, to check, to keep under control, to restrain. It can be a temporary act.

Reported	Corrected
It was decided ***to repress*** the anarchist publication because it incited violence.	It was decided **to suppress** the anarchist publication because it incited violence.
All advice and talk he hears at home ***suppresses*** his ambition to become a monk.	All advice and talk he hears at home **represses** his ambition to become a monk.

184 – Sympathy or Empathy?

Sympathy is compassion, a feeling for another person's sorrow. It can also mean support for another person's viewpoint or stand taken against some authority.

Empathy is not a new word but it began to be used widely in the 1980s. It is stronger and deeper than **sympathy** and relates not only to sadness but to other emotions. The feelings twins have for one another – in some cases their identical reactions and achievements – may be described as **empathy.**

The origin of **empathy** is said to be a German philosophical word meaning sympathetic understanding, fellow feeling. The sympathiser becomes part of the sorrow or emotion, taking a greater share than sympathy might suggest. We have **sympathy for someone** and **empathy with someone.**

When EMPATHY is deeper than SYMPATHY
My sister died in a car accident a year ago. Yesterday my closest friend, Joan, lost her brother in a similar disaster. My feelings are more than **sympathy** for my friend. They are **empathy** with her. It is as if it had happened to me again.

185 – Tenses wrongly mixed

The tenses of verbs in a sentence should balance. **Present follows present** and **past follows past** if the time of the action is the same. The intended meaning, however, is seldom destroyed when tenses are wrongly mixed but the result is ugly to the eye and understanding is less easy.

PAST and PRESENT

Wrong	Corrected
When *I suggested* a date and place to him, *he refuses* to discuss it.	When **I suggested** a date and place to him, **he refused** to discuss it.
I shall read the magazine *if I bought it.*	**I shall read** the magazine **if I buy it.**
When we *played* tennis today, we *see* Concorde flying across the Channel.	When we **played** tennis today, we **saw** Concorde flying across the Channel.

DOUBLE PAST

Wrong	Corrected
I expected *to have seen* you.	I expected **to see** you.
I wanted *to have gone* to Eye *to have taken* your advice.	I wanted **to go** to Eye **to take** your advice.
They were prepared *to have spent* more than £1000 on the antique.	They were prepared **to spend** more than £1000 on the antique.

SHALL with WILL   SHOULD with WOULD

Wrong	Corrected
I *should* be grateful if you *will* repair the roof of the parish hall.	I **should** be grateful if you **would** repair the roof of the parish hall.
We *shall* be delighted if you *would* perform the opening ceremony.	We **shall** be delighted if you **will** perform the opening ceremony.

186 – Than she or Than her? As I or As me?

Eminent grammarians have discussed the use of **than** and **as** in many excellent manuals published over the last fifty years, but the endless grammatical terms have confused some of us. *Make No Mistake* looks only at the area where doubt and misunderstanding are noticed most.

Both words are conjunctions (than **she** is, as **they** are). But many modern grammarians claim that they also function as prepositions (than **her,** as **them)** and therein are the problems.

(1) After conjunctions we write: **I/he/she/we/they.** "He has more money **than I** (have). He is as fit **as I** (am)." *(They are known as subjective pronouns)*

(2) After prepositions: **me/him/her/us/them.** "He has more cash **than me.** He is as fit **as me.**" *(Objective pronouns)*

The advice offered in most linguistic circles is to regard (1) as formal and strictly correct and (2) as less pedantic and more acceptable, even if it is to be labelled colloquial.

When a verb follows **than I** (also **he/she/we/they**), whether actually written or implied, errors are unlikely. That, of course, also applies to **as I.** One grammarian consulted said that he teaches use of the implied verb that could follow:

They keep more horses than **we do** **(or keep).**

He has seen much more of Europe than **I have.**

She is undoubtedly as clever **as he** **is.**

They are as busy in their factory **as we** **are.**

Much of the conversation we hear ignores the traditional grammar, with **as** and **than** used as prepositions. Clarity as well as conformity is required, and extra words or re-writing a sentence can sometimes be the only answer to doubt and difficulty. Care has to be taken to avoid misunderstanding.

Ambiguous: The manager praised Sarah as much as me.

Re-written: The manager praised Sarah as much as he praised me.

OR: The manager praised Sarah as much as I did.

Sylvia Chalker in her *English Grammar Word by Word* asks: What does the following mean?

She loves her home more than her husband.

It could mean "She loves her home more than her husband loves it", or "She loves her home more than she loves him."

187 – There or Their?

The mistake seen occasionally is ***there*** for **their** – probably through thoughtlessness rather than ignorance. The appalling error, however, did appear in a highly respected publication; in that case, obviously through ignorant choice of ***there*** and not the result of a printer's error.

There: Pointing in the direction of some place or object, or calling attention to something. **"There is** no cheese, only butter, on the table **over there."**

Their: Indicates that they have possession. **"Their horses** have already left the racecourse for **their stables."**

Wrong	Corrected
They are reducing ***there services*** and increasing ***there weekly fees. Their is*** no sense in that.	They are reducing **their services** and increasing **their weekly fees. There is** no sense in that.

188 – This, That, These, Those

All four words usually mention persons or things without naming them, and careless writing sometimes fails to identify precisely the noun to which reference is made.

This denotes somebody or something which is about to be or has just been mentioned. **These** is the plural. **That** may be more distant in time and place than **this,** although there are many cases where they are interchangeable. **Those** is the plural.

"This (hammer) is yours. **That** (a dog in the field) is John Soper's. **These** (books) are not for sale. They lived in Cornwall for ten years; **those** were the best years of their lives."

Meaning not clear	Corrected
A German orchestra will be engaged to play two Beethoven symphonies. ****This*** is the committee's decision, against the President's wish.	The committee has decided, against the President's wish, to engage a German orchestra, which will play the two Beethoven symphonies.

**This refers to the preference for a German orchestra, not to the decision to play two Beethoven symphonies.*

189 – Try TO repair or Try AND repair?

Not a day passes when *Try and go* or its equivalent is not seen in print or heard on radio and television. It is wrong and cannot be supported, although defenders of *try and find* shelter behind "It's colloquial, it's idiomatic". Consider:

> Krish will **try and repair** the car tomorrow.

What will he try? Will he try to find the time to repair the car? Will he try to find the right tools to repair the car? We are not told. *He will try and* has now become so common that it is obvious that Krish **will try to repair it.**

Substitute three synonyms for try – attempt, endeavour and strive. The misuse of *and* for **to** becomes even more unacceptable. Who would write or say:

> Will he attempt AND repair the car tomorrow?
>
> Will he endeavour AND repair the car tomorrow?
>
> Will he strive AND repair the car tomorrow?

Apart from consideration of grammar, **to** in place of *and* makes sense and expresses what is meant. That is illustrated clearly when a negative is written. "He will *not try and repair* the car" instead of "He will **not try to repair** the car".

Wrong	Corrected
I shall try and go to Gordon's Bay for my holiday next August.	**I shall try to go** to Gordon's Bay for my holiday next August.
They will attempt and climb Mount Everest if the money needed can be found.	**They will attempt to climb** Mount Everest if the money needed can be found.
It will be sad if *they try and persuade* James not to take the job.	It will be sad if **they try to persuade** James not to take the job.
I shall not try and run the full marathon again in London next year.	**I shall not try to run** the full marathon again in London next year.

Exceptions, with **and** following try, are seen when a pause requires a comma. "Are you going to mend it?" – "I shall try, **and** you shall see the result". "You want me to sing. I shall try, **and** you will not forget it!"

190 – Unanimous or Nem. con.?

In **a unanimous decision** everyone votes for a proposal. A jury may produce **a unanimous verdict** to convict a person charged with burglary. The adjective is broadly defined as showing that views or sentiments are shared. The noun **unanimity** indicates full agreement in opinion or purpose.

Nem. con. is the Latin abbreviation for *nemine contradicente,* meaning no one was against a proposal, although some did not vote. It should not be confused with **majority,** which could mean that eight voted in favour and seven against.

Wrong	Corrected
We passed the plan ***unanimously.*** Twenty voted in favour; only two did not vote.	We passed the plan **nem. con.** Twenty voted in favour; only two did not vote.
The jury found the defendant guilty on a vote that was ***nem. con.,*** only two voting against the verdict.	The jury found the defendant guilty on a vote that was **not unanimous,** as two voted against the verdict.

191 – United Kingdom or Great Britain?

Mistakes reflect a writer's frailty in matters geographical and historical, but accurate distinction is necessary in many English language documents and reports.

The **United Kingdom** comprises England, Scotland, Wales and Northern Ireland – not the Channel Islands or the Isle of Man, which are direct Crown dependencies. **Great Britain** is England, Scotland and Wales, making up the largest island in Europe.

Wrong	Corrected
Belfast, capital of Northern Ireland, has one of ***Great Britain's*** busiest ports.	**Belfast,** capital of Northern Ireland, has one of the **United Kingdom's** busiest ports.

The **British Isles** consists of Great Britain, Ireland (the Republic and Northern Ireland), the Channel Islands and the Isle of Man – separated from the mainland of Europe by the North Sea and the English Channel. The Channel tunnel now links Great Britain to Europe.

192 – Unsatisfied or Dissatisfied?

Dissatisfied shows displeasure at something offered, received or felt. A motorist becomes discontented with a new car and tells the sales' manager that he is **dissatisfied.**

A person may be dissatisfied with a meal at a restaurant because the courses were small and his hunger was **unsatisfied.**

Reported	Preferred
All 80 books were sold on Monday within two hours of arrival, leaving dozens of callers ***dissatisfied.***	All 80 books were sold on Monday within two hours of arrival, leaving dozens of callers **unsatisfied** – and **dissatisfied.**
I could not have been more ***unsatisfied*** with a choir. There was not a balance of voices and they often sang out of tune.	I could not have been more **dissatisfied** with a choir. There was not a balance of voices and they often sang out of tune.

193 – Wage or Salary?

Gardener wanted for Perthshire country house: **good wage.** That is an advertisement. The employee will cultivate a garden and be paid weekly. **Wages** are paid to such persons, known as blue-collar workers, **for manual work.**

Qualified accountant required for city practice: **salary negotiable** (advertisement). He or she will probably be paid monthly at an agreed annual rate. That is the normal arrangement for those who provide professional services. They are known as the salaried classes, or white-collar workers.

Changes, however, are taking place, as **wage is seen by many as a mark of class distinction.** The modern word-fashion is to state earnings per week or rate per hour, without the word **wage.**

Not advertised	Advertised
Chartered surveyors require office manager. ***Wage*** in line with age and experience.	Chartered surveyors require office manager. **Salary** in line with age and experience.

194 – Whether/Whether or/Whether or not?

1 – **Whether** alone in a sentence is usually an alternative to **if** and is preferred when posing a question or doubt about a possibility. Example:

He hasn't decided yet **whether (if)** he should go to the fair.

After a preposition (to, on etc), **write whether,** not *if.* Example:

My job depends on **whether** the company wins the contract.

2 – **Whether...or** identifies alternatives in a sentence.

I question **whether** the company's chairman objects to the sale of the factory **or** is taking action to stop it.

Make No Mistake follows the principle that, where the possibilities are opposites, **whether** should be repeated, as in this example (rejects and acceptance being opposites):

I do not know whether your company rejects our offer **or whether** acceptance is delayed.

3 – **Whether** can be followed by **or not** when two opposites are considered.

Whether you play **or not**, I shall be there.

Whether you settle part of the debt today **or not**, a court order will be obtained.

Reported	Corrected
George will tell you tonight ***whether or not*** he can take his holiday next week or must wait until next month.	George will tell you tonight **whether** he can take his holiday next week **or** must wait until next month.
I doubt ***whether or not*** we can pay the price you are asking for the donkey.	I doubt **whether** we can pay the price you are asking for the donkey.
Whether Judy obtains a high-speed shorthand certificate, she is certain to be appointed to a senior secretarial post.	**Whether** Judy obtains a high-speed shorthand certificate **or not,** she is certain to be appointed to a senior secretarial post.

195 – Who or Whom?

Those who say that grammar doesn't matter, so long as the listener or reader understands, will probably declare **whom** to be dead. But **whom** is alive and cannot be buried. The rule for its use may be paraphrased briefly as follows:

Who is written when it is the SUBJECT of a verb, as in

The engineer who repaired the lorry was your friend Parker.

The young man who helped you works for me.

In both cases, **who** is related to the person who does or has done something.

Whom is written when it is the OBJECT of a verb.

John Smithson, **whom everyone respects**, speaks next. (*Everyone respects* **him**)

Who has evolved, to be accepted widely, as a replacement for **whom** in many cases, especially in questions, even though it is contrary to formal grammar.

"*Who* did you see last night?" has usurped "**Whom** did you see last night?"

Four suggestions may help to clear doubting minds:

1 – To determine whether it is correct to use **who** or **whom,** re-phrase the sentence with **I/we/he/she/they** for **who** and rephrase it with **me/him/her/us/them** for **whom** to convey the same meaning. Examples:

We saw the President, **who** inspected a guard of honour.

We saw the President; **he** ***(not him,*** therefore ***not whom)*** inspected a guard of honour.

The author is Dick Francis, **whom** I judge to be one of the most successful of our time.

The author is Dick Francis; I judge **him** (not ***he,*** not ***who***) to be one of the most successful of our time.

2 – When a question begins with **who,** the answer, if it is to start with a pronoun, will be **I, he, she, we** or **they.** Example:

Who will play the organ tonight? **She will.**

Similarly, the response to **whom** in the form of a question will be **me, him, her, us** or **them.** Example:

Whom do you expect today? **Them.**

Exchange **whom** for **me, him, her, us** or **them** to confirm the proper use of **whom.** Example:

Whom did you ask? EXCHANGED – Did you ask **him?**

It has to be conceded that, in speech at any rate, the question would probably be phrased "Who do you expect today?"

3 – A preposition **(to, for, about** etc.) must be followed by **whom,** not ***who.*** Examples:

The neighbours gave a new chair to the old man, **for whom** they had great affection.

About whom do you wish to write in this week's article?

One grammarian advises that "The neighbours gave a new chair to the old man ***who they had great affection for***" is equally acceptable. That is rejected here in the belief that the first example above looks better, sounds better and is grammatically impeccable.

4 – **Who** ***(not whom)*** should be written with the verb to be **(am, was, were** etc). Examples:

He knows **who you are.** Do you know **who I am?**

Wrong	Corrected
** We like the English teacher ***who you criticised*** so fiercely yesterday. *** The thief ***whom I am told took*** your car is well known to the police.	** We like the English teacher **whom you criticised** so fiercely yesterday. *** The thief **who, I am told, took** your car is well known to the police.

** NOTE: It is common usage now, especially in speech, to delete **whom,** leaving us with "We know the teacher you criticise so fiercely".

NOTE: The commonsense of grammar is seen when "I am told" is taken out of both sentences – **who took,** not ***whom took.

196 – Who/Which or That?

Reported: The Brock picture of Jane, that is at least 150 years old, has been sold to an American dealer. Wrong. **Which,** not ***that,*** should be written at the beginning of a clause when it needs a comma at each end.

The clause – **"which is at least 150 years old"** – provides extra information and is known as NON-DEFINING. (Note: **Which** is for things and **who** is for people). A sentence still makes sense without the words between the commas. Examples:

> Dr Smith, ***who is 75,*** still cares for his patients.
>
> Our son, ***who is a virologist,*** has just returned from China.

Which, who or **that** without commas *(below)* provide essential meaning if no deliberate pause is needed when spoken. Hence the term DEFINING CLAUSE:

> The doctor ***who (or that) answers calls promptly*** is my son.
>
> Here is the horse ***that made so much money.***

The clauses in italics are essential to the sentences if they are to convey intended meanings. They are clearly defining.

The importance of good punctuation is apparent when defining and non-defining clauses are considered. A comma omitted or wrongly placed can change meaning.

> All the prisoners who had earned remission of their sentences for good behaviour went home today.

Without commas after **prisoners** and **behaviour,** some prisoners were released. With commas, all prisoners would have gone home.

Reported (note the commas)	Corrected
My old clock |,| ***that*** is worth a fortune, will be sold at auction next week.	My old clock |,| **which** is worth a fortune, will be sold at auction next week.
The Taj Mahal which I saw many years ago stands out in my memory.	**The Taj Mahal** |,| **which** I saw many years ago |,| stands out in my memory.
You cannot sell ***a car*** |,| ***that*** has a broken axle and three worn-out tyres.	You cannot sell **a car that** has a broken axle and three worn-out tyres.

197 – Without

One definition of **without** is externally, outside. That is an adverb, seldom used. As a preposition it means free from, in the absence of, dispense with. The main reason for its inclusion here is that it should not be written, except as a colloquialism, for the conjunction ***unless.***

Wrong	Corrected
We shall ***never*** buy another thing in that shop ***without*** they introduce a higher standard of cleanliness.	We shall **not** buy another thing in that shop **unless** they introduce a higher standard of cleanliness.

198 – Words distorted

A number of words are given an unnatural meaning, mainly in speech. The use of some has expanded to mean **very,** but they defy the Queen's English for many of us. **Frightfully** is defined as terribly and shockingly, yet we hear it applied with the opposite sense. Examples of words classed here as distortions, often spoken but seldom written:

Fearfully **ignorant.** ***Awfully*** **nice.** ***Terrific*** **meal.**

Frightfully **pleasant.** ***Beastly*** **shame.** ***Dreadfully*** **tired.**

Tremendously **funny.** **A** ***regular*** **fool.** ***Perfectly*** **ridiculous.**

He is a ***terribly*** **nice person.** **They made a** ***decent*** **profit.**

Most of us have words we dislike and rarely write. **Nice** is one of them. It seldom gives anything a clear description. The *Shorter Oxford English Dictionary* (two volumes) traces its origins to ignorant, which is missing from today's wide range of definitions: fastidious, particular, delicately sensitive, subtle, exact, pleasing, agreeable, scrupulous, requiring precision, minute, attractive and so on. The most acceptable, perhaps, are **pleasing, attractive** and **agreeable.**

Nice is often part of a colloquialism – **A nice mess; a nice load of rubbish; a nice villain.** It has become a word used when the writer's mind fails to find an appropriate one. It is not truly descriptive, as seen here:

She is a **nice lady** who lives in that nice house on the hill.

The lady, in fact, is attractive and the house is a ten-room Georgian mansion.

199 – Words with a Hyphen

Hyphens should not be confused with the dash. They are shorter, although most typewriters and word processors have only one symbol for both.

They link syllables and words (ink-pot, non-profitability, twenty-one). Dashes are used to keep words and phrases apart, usually marking an afterthought or explanation in the middle or at the end of a sentence.

The hyphen prevents misunderstanding in the description of a person, animal or object. Note the possible change of meaning in these two sentences:

A British car salesman joins us in Paris *(He is British).*

A British-car salesman joins us in Paris *(Appointed to sell British cars).*

That long suffering reptile *(A long snake. It suffers).*

That long-suffering reptile *(It suffered for a long time).*

The general rule is to use the hyphen where it helps the reader, even if no confusion is likely. Examples:

A hard-working plumber.	**T-shirt.**	**Wild-cat strike.**
The four-year-old boy.	**Ex-directory.**	**A medium-sized car.**

Compound words are less of a problem because two forms are accepted for many of them. Pre-historic is now authentic as **prehistoric,** take-over as **takeover,** wind-pipe as **windpipe,** by-pass as **bypass** etc. How long before cross-examination becomes **crossexamination?** But spare us from compound words that stretch into 30 or 40 letters as in German!

MEANINGS change if the hyphen is omitted

re-creation *(create anew)*	**recreation** *(pastime, amusement, exercise at play)*
re-count *(count again)*	**recount** *(to narrate)*
re-form *(form again)*	**reform** *(to remove faults, amend)*
re-sign *(sign again)*	**resign** *(give up, retire, submit)*
re-cover *(replace a cover)*	**recover** *(regain, get well again, revive, retrieve)*
re-lay *(lay again)*	**relay** *(one worker or runner relieves another)*

200 – Words wasted

A wide vocabulary enables writers to select words and phrases that convey their thoughts simply and directly. When they edit their reports, essays or memoranda, opportunities to economise in wordage are almost always seen.

One of the superfluous phrases in the English language is ***in order to.*** The meaning becomes sharper as well as shorter when ***in order*** is deleted, although one grammarian makes the point that it sometimes "clarifies and disambiguates".

Reported	Preferred
She was aiming to try to become a good shorthand writer.	**Her aim was** to become a good shorthand writer.
There are some circumstances ***in which*** your excuse would be accepted.	In some circumstances your excuse would be accepted.
I am going to Glasgow ***in order to buy*** a gold bracelet.	I am going to Glasgow **to buy** a gold bracelet.
Interest rates are going up ***in order to try*** to curb inflation.	Interest rates are going up **to try** to curb inflation.
He sends his ***grateful thanks.***	He sends his **thanks**
They have started ***felling down*** the trees in our road.	They have started **felling** the trees in our road.
Our best tennis player is always aiming ***to try to become*** the county champion.	Our best tennis player is always **aiming at becoming** the county champion.
Of all the antiques we saw at the exhibition, that Chippendale chair was ***the best of them all.***	Of all the antiques we saw at the exhibition, that Chippendale chair was **the best.**
Manchester and Edinburgh differ greatly in environment ***from each other.***	Manchester and Edinburgh differ greatly in environment.
There is a lot that could be said in favour of the scheme you are sending to the chairman.	**A lot could be said** in favour of the scheme you are sending to the chairman.

Spelling

Two Hundred and fifty words that head the list of common mistakes

Spelling depends almost entirely on a good memory and keeping a dictionary at hand. Pronunciation is not a reliable guide. Many words are spoken alike but have different meanings. They are known as homonyms. Examples among two or three hundred:

principle/principal	draft/draught	bear/bare
knight/night	meat/meet	main/mane
site/sight/cite	cereal/serial	fair/fare
stationary/stationery	beer/bier	roll/role

There are reminders that aid good spelling. In words requiring **ei** or **ie**, the **i** usually comes before the **e** except after **c.** Examples:

piece	believe	relieve	mischief	retrieve
receive	deceit	conceive	conceited	ceiling

But that is not an absolute rule. There are inconsistencies:

weird	seize	deficiency	sufficiency	counterfeit

An extra **n** is needed when words that start with **n**, such as **necessary, natural, noticed, noble, numerable, numbered, nerve** and **neighbourly** are converted into the negative:

unnecessary	unnatural	unnoticed	ennoble
innumerable	unnumbered	unnerve	unneighbourly

Similarly, an extra **l** and an extra **r** are written when reversing the meaning of words beginning with **il** and **ir**:

illegible	illegal	illiterate	illegitimate
irregular	irrelevant	irreversible	irrevocable

The double **ss** is part of the negative in **satisfied, service** and **similar: dissatisfied, disservice, dissimilar.**

One problem is left largely to writers, namely: Should we use **-ize** or **-ise** in the verbs ***economize, organize, criticize, realize*** etc? The author opted for **-ise** long ago, although there are exceptions. *(See No. 112 in Common Mistakes.)*

The emphasis in many schools and colleges on writing creative, imaginative language, regardless of all else, may have weakened the importance of spelling. The claim that to be understood is the main and, possibly, the only object, leads to acceptance of these offerings as satisfactory:

> If the skylark ***sored*** (soared), the meaning is clear enough.
>
> You can expect them ***hear*** (here) later today.
>
> If the ***accomodation*** (accommodation) is all right, why worry about the second **m**?

That thinking is rejected here, as it has been by recent Secretaries of State for Education in the United Kingdom.

Journalists should be among the best spellers, but almost 300 different words were misspelt when 165 young reporters sat an examination. Examples *(see corrections in ABC list below)*:

definate	***arguement***	***critism***	***reguarded***
exagerated	***sentenace***	***variaty***	***discription***
existance	***vertually***	***propoganda***	***jepardy***

A group of trainee-secretaries, working without dictionaries, produced a rare assortment of mistakes from dictation:

substanciary	***committment***	***fullfilled***	***accomodation***
substancially	***commited***	***forfilled***	***accomadation***
redundencies	***restaurent***	***expence***	***reccomended***
rediculus	***resturant***	***sored***	***obviousley***

ADVICE: Concentrate on your twenty most troublesome words. Bank them in the memory by writing them repeatedly as an exercise until they form a clear mental picture of the word. Start with **separate** and **occurred.** Writing anything is the best aid to memory.

THE TEN MISTAKES most commonly seen, with corrections in brackets, taken from letters, documents, theses, advertising brochures and other publications, are listed in order of frequent occurrence:

1 – ***seperate***	(separate)	6 – ***reccomend***	(recommend)
2 – ***accomodate***	(accommodate)	7 – ***prefered***	(preferred)
3 – ***occured***	(occurred)	8 – ***transfered***	(transferred)
4 – ***beleived***	(believed)	9 – ***occassion***	(occasion)
5 – ***recieved***	(received)	10 – ***benefitted***	(benefited)

Spelling mistakes in almost all areas of communication, some of them in official letters or papers, were noted during research into spelling for *Make No Mistake* (see alternatives in *Amercian Variations*). Some were as common as those shown on p.172.

Common mistake	Correct
Abhorrant	Abhorrent
abscence	absence
accellerate	accelerate
accidently	accidentally
aquited	acquitted
admissable	admissible
alloted	allotted
alluminum	aluminium
amitter	amateur
anesethic	anaesthetic
anonymus	anonymous
appealling	appealing
apprechiate	appreciate
arguement	argument
assasinate	assassinate
assistent	assistant
Barbeque	barbecue
bargin	bargain
behavior	behaviour
bigotted	bigoted
Brittania	Britannia
Budha	Buddha
budgetted	budgeted
bisiness	business
Canceled	cancelled
catagories	categories
catalog	catalogue
cattarrh	catarrh
cemitry	cemetery
changable	changeable
chargable	chargeable
cocoanut	coconut
collossal	colossal
comemorate	commemorate
commited	committed
comittee	committee
committment	commitment
comparitively	comparatively
computor	computer
concieve	conceive
condence	condense
contanent	continent
consientious	conscientious
coroborate	corroborate
counterfiet	counterfeit
couragous	courageous
critism	criticism
customery	customary
couriosity	curiosity
Decieved	Deceived
defense	defence
definate	definite
defishinsy	deficiency
desparate	desperate
dissapoint	disappoint
dispondent	despondent
disatisfied	dissatisfied
distill	distil
develope	develop
delapedated	dilapidated
discription	description
dispise	despise
disapear	disappear
disasterous	disastrous
descriminate	discriminate
disimilar	dissimilar
Earlyest	Earliest
editer	editor
embarassment	embarrassment
elegible	eligible
enforcable	enforceable
enormus	enormous
enrollment	enrolment
intrust	entrust
equater	equator
equivelant	equivalent
equiped	equipped
exagerate	exaggerate
exadurate	
exsess	excess

Common mistake	Correct
excercise	exercise
excell	excel
existance	existence
exhorbitant	exorbitant
expence	expense
extravegent	extravagant
Fasinate	Fascinate
favor	favour
feasable	feasible
Febuary	February
flavor	flavour
flexable	flexible
foollish	foolish
forstal	forestall
freind	friend
fullfil	fulfil
fullfilled	fulfilled
fulfillment	fulfilment
Gibralter	Gibraltar
glammer	glamour
goverment	government
grammer	grammar
grievence	grievance
gratefull	grateful
guarentee	guarantee
gymnaisiom	gymnasium
Haemhorrage	Haemorrhage
headake	headache
harbor	harbour
harrass	harass
humerous	humorous
Illegable	Illegible
immiately	immediately
iminent	imminent
increese	increase
indefensable	indefensible
indelable	indelible
independance	independence
indispensible	indispensable
inexhaustable	inexhaustible
infered	inferred
inflamable	inflammable
enfuse	infuse

Common mistake	Correct
innoculate	inoculate
inocuous	innocuous
Keeness	Keenness
Labeled	Labelled
labor	labour
lemenade	lemonade
leval	level
libary	library
Maintainence	Maintenance
managable	manageable
maneuver	manoeuvre
marraige	marriage
marvelous	marvellous
mustached	moustache
Mediteranean	Mediterranean
mearly	merely
meteorlogical	meteorological
minature	miniature
mischeivous	mischievous
misalanios	miscellaneous
misstake	mistake
morgage	mortgage
moveable	movable
Nescessary	Necessary
neglegable	negligible
neighbor	neighbour
noteable	notable
noticable	noticeable
nuisence	nuisance
Obviousley	Obviously
occurence	occurrence
offense	offence
omited	omitted
orchestrer	orchestra
Pajamas	pyjamas
pavillion	pavilion
paralell	parallel

Common mistake	Correct	Common mistake	Correct
Parliment	Parliament	***Satallite***	Satellite
parrafin	paraffin	***sieze***	seize
patiant	patient	***sence***	sense
penecillin	penicillin	***sensative***	sensitive
permissable	permissible	***sentance***	sentence
pursuade	persuade	***seige***	siege
peice	piece	***skillfull***	skilful
pianoes	pianos	***substancially***	substantially
posession	possession	***successfull***	successful
potatos	potatoes	***sufficiant***	sufficient
preceed	precede	***superintendant***	superintendent
prevelent	prevalent		
primative	primitive	***Tarrif***	Tariff
priviledge	privilege	***tecknical***	technical
procede	proceed	***tempory***	temporary
prosession	procession	***tabacco***	tobacco
proffession	profession	***tomatos***	tomatoes
proferred	proffered	***traveling***	travelling
propoganda	propaganda		
perchase	purchase	***Unforgetable***	Unforgettable
persue	pursue	***unanamous***	unanimous
		unessessary	unnecessary
Quareled	Quarrelled	***unparallelled***	unparalleled
		untill	until
Reciept	Receipt	***useable***	usable
redundencies	redundancies		
refered	referred	***Variaty***	Variety
regretable	regrettable	***vengance***	vengeance
reguarded	regarded	***verticle***	vertical
relagate	relegate	***veterinery***	veterinary
releaved	relieved		
reminescent	reminiscent	***Wierd***	Weird
repitition	repetition	***weild***	wield
resistence	resistance	***withold***	withhold
responsability	responsibility	***woolen***	woollen
resturant	restaurant	***worshiped***	worshipped
rediculous	ridiculous		

The Sunday Times (1991) conducted a survey into educational standards among children aged 10 or 11 and reported: "Children in Britain's classrooms cannot spell simple words because schools are abandoning traditional methods of teaching and testing".

They found an exception at Roecliffe Church of England primary near Boroughbridge in North Yorkshire, where pupils had short spelling tests every Monday and Friday. If a child spelt a word wrongly in written work, it was corrected at the bottom of the page and then learnt off by heart. All the children had words in a folder which they made into punctuated sentences.

American variations

The American influence on the English language has to be recognised. ***Program*** instead of **programme** now appears not only in the United States but worldwide; in relation to computers, **program** is a universal word. There should be a common base in spelling, but many alternatives have become acceptable.

American spelling follows the phonetics more closely than the original structure. The aim is simplicity, which is seen in the single use of **practise** and **licence**, instead of **practice** *(noun)*/**practise** *(verb)* and **licence** *(noun)*/**license** *(verb)*.

The most common American variations, with British spelling in brackets:

aluminum *(aluminium)*
anesthetic *(anaesthetic)*
appall *(appal)*
armor *(armour)*

behavior *(behaviour)*

catalog *(catalogue)*
center *(centre)*
check *(cheque)*
cigaret *(cigarette)*
color *(colour)*

defense *(defence)*
dike *(dyke)*
encyclopedia *(encyclopaedia)*
enrollment *(enrolment)*

favor *(favour)*
fiber *(fibre)*
flavor *(flavour)*
fulfill *(fulfil)*
fulfillment *(fulfilment)*

harbor *(harbour)*
honor *(honour)*

inclose *(enclose)*
indorse *(endorse)*

installment *(instalment)*
instill *(instil)*
intrust *(entrust)*

labor *(labour)*
a license *(a licence)*
liter *(litre)*

maneuver *(manoeuvre)*
marvelous *(marvellous)*
meter *(metre)*
miter *(mitre)*
mustache *(moustache)*

neighbor *(neighbour)*
offense *(offence)*

pajamas *(pyjamas)*
plow *(plough)*
to practice *(to practise)*
pretense *(pretence)*
program *(programme)*

skillful *(skilful)*
splendor *(splendour)*

sulfur *(sulphur)*

tire *(tyre)*

Erratum

P176,2nd paragraph, read: use of PRACTICE (not practise) and LICENSE (not licence)

THE LAST WORD

Everyone who has read some, most or all of *Make No Mistake* will have recognised the variations in and interpretations of our language. A distinguished teacher of English to foreign nationals for more than 40 years closes the book with a plea he has long been making — one which the author supports.

The case for an English language authority — not to dictate but to recommend

By Geoffrey Kitchin FIL FRSA

We need, we must have, an English Language Academy. Beyond fulfilling a number of essential purposes, it would be recognisable from abroad and would sustain our English in the face of pressures from others.

It could establish one grammar and thus eliminate subjectivity and argument, provide a firmer teaching base and answer foreign calls for logic and order. It might issue criticisms of malpractices and promote initiatives conducive to good English. It would not, could not, dictate; but it would provide information and recommendation to all who sought them. The French Academy should not be seen as a model; we are different people, and our languages have different problems.

I see the English Language Academy as a body set up and funded like a government agency. As such it would immediately attract universal respect. With two-thirds of the world's population now claiming English as their first or second language, we have lost much authority over it, and we need to regain control.

The ELA might be a two-tier council. The lower would be made up of English experts with first-hand experience of the specialised fields of industry, commerce, sciences and the arts; it would be both watchdog and consultant. The upper tier would incorporate representatives of the arts (literature, poetry, theatre, music), an etymologist, a terminologist and a modern linguist; it would debate the finer points of the language and be decision-making. One chairman could preside over both.

Traditionally, the yardstick by which we have measured Standard English has been usage: common, respected, accepted, call it what you like. This has been a cosy policy, in keeping with our British dislike of regulation and our easy-going national character. However, the effectiveness of usage, so variously interpreted in so many cultures, has become highly questionable.

At home, if usage is seen as "common", the proletarianised versions spoken by large proportions of our people, are at once given validity; if "respected", what credence can you then give to usage in a society which speaks in terms of self-interest, hooliganism, vandalism and violence? And if "accepted", what value can you attribute to it in an age of permissiveness when anything goes? How, in these circumstances, can usage enjoy any sort of authority?

Our Continental neighbours compare English with their own languages, which are orderly and fortified against alien influences by a single logical set of rules established by a recognised authority. "Your English has no rules", they complain. "One teacher says this, another says that, they rarely agree! If you have rules, who makes them?" They are right, of course: the validity of rules depends on the measure of respect accorded to the rule-maker.

Would it not be better for our children if teachers shared a uniform view of the structural backbone of the language, based on rules and principles agreed and formulated by an English Language Academy? Usage would not be discarded – quite the contrary, it is only under the protection of an academy that it will survive.

We in Britain urgently need to provide visible proof that we are intent on safeguarding our culture. Only then shall we be able in the end to pass on our inherited language to our heirs and successors, satisfied in the knowledge that we have done what was necessary to preserve it for them.

INDEX